A Broken Propeller

A Broken Propeller

BAZ BAGBY
AND AMERICA'S FIRST
TRANSCONTINENTAL AIR RACE

BETTY GOERKE

WASHINGTON DC

Library of Congress Control Number: 2017956931
ISBN 978-0-9986433-9-7 paperback (alk. paper)

Book and cover design and composition by Beth Hansen-Winter

 An imprint of New Academia Publishing

 New Academia Publishing
4401-A Connecticut Ave. NW, #236, Washington, DC 20008
info@newacademia.com; www.newacademia.com

COVER: **DH-4 over France, WWI. Detroit Public Library.**

TO MY LOVING FATHER,
RALPH "BAZ" BAGBY

CONTENTS

88th Observation Squadron, September, 1918. U.S. Air Service.

Lt. Baz Bagby first row, sixth from left.

The broken propeller with three of Baz's four great-grandchildren:
Jane, Jack, and Ben Bagby, 2016.

PREFACE:
THE PROPELLER

*W*HEN I GREW UP in Evanston, Illinois, there was a broken propeller from a World War I plane in our basement. It had moved with my Dad and Mom from Langley Field, Virginia, where my father was stationed as a pilot from 1919–21, to civilian life in Iowa, to apartments in Evanston, and finally to a house with a basement big enough to accommodate it properly. As a kid I knew my Dad had played pro baseball, had ridden the rails, and graduated from the Massachusetts Institute of Technology. But I knew little about his WWI adventures in a plane over enemy lines, and nothing at all about the mysterious, unexplained broken propeller. I do remember vividly the radio announcement on December 7, 1941, of the bombing of Pearl Harbor, and the mournful string quartet that was playing when my Dad came home from a golf game and stated that he would volunteer as a pilot with the U.S. Army Air Corps. When he returned from the war in 1945, I was well aware of his exploits, including his D-Day adventure, in which he went AWOL and pulled rank as a colonel in order to jump alongside young parachutists behind enemy lines just hours before the air assault and troop landing on the French beaches. At the end of the war, he flew French Jewish prisoners, newly released from Buchenwald, back to Paris.

My father, Ralph Bagby, grew up in New Haven, Missouri, a small town where time was marked by the whistle of the train that went through twice a day. Born in 1893, the third oldest of 12 children, he and all of his brothers worked at the family tree nursery behind their home, high on the bluffs above the Missouri River.

As a father he read us the funny papers, played the mandolin, sang songs he had learned from former slaves, and told us tales from Greek history. Before the Second World War he would hide treats in his hands when he came home from work. "Blind your eyes," he would say as we reached out trying to tap the hand with the treat. Often my father would ask me to pick out tunes on the piano that we had listened to on the radio. "Your Hit Parade" was a favorite radio show on Saturday night. I played and we sang "Somewhere Over the Rainbow" and "Chattanooga Choo Choo." When Dad came home for a short visit during WWII we sang "Don't Sit Under the Apple Tree." During his three-and-a-half years of overseas service in WWII Dad wrote us charming letters filled with stories, and admonitions to mind our mom.

After the War, when I was in high school, I became aware that my father was a unique character: smiling, unassuming, a storyteller, loving and beloved, a friend of both blue-collar workers and Winston Churchill. His given name was Ralph, but he was known affectionately as Baz, and people would smile when they said his name.

In 2012, long after the deaths of my parents, I returned to the family home in Evanston, where my brother Jay introduced me to a tiny, musty closet whose entry required crawling on hands and knees. Here, tucked away, were letters and photographs of our father's war experiences, as well as his flight log, WWI aviator's uniform, and Mom's 1920 wedding dress. Reading Dad's letters as they were hauled out box by box, I learned for the first time about the Transcontinental Air Race of 1919. At the time I thought it would be fun to write a whimsical account of his experiences in the race, along the lines of "Those Daring Young Men in Their Flying Machines." It wasn't until I read contemporary news reports and official U.S. Army documents about the purpose and details of the race that I saw another side of the competition: a historically important portrayal of a dangerous, hastily planned adventure.

➤ INTRODUCTION ◄

*I*N OCTOBER 1919, a spectacular event took place across America. The round-trip race of 59 World War I planes with open cockpits and no parachutes began simultaneously on Long Island and in San Francisco with 22 predetermined stops. Few people know of the race today, but at the time it was followed closely by the press with front-page headlines announcing who was ahead, who was missing, who made an unexpected emergency landing, who crashed, and who fell victim to blinding snowstorms.

Many of the pilots were World War I heroes, having risked their lives just months earlier in the skies of France over German-held territory. They welcomed peace and knew they were lucky to be alive, but life seemed dull without the constant challenge of battle. The Transcontinental Air Race provided a new challenge. It was the brainchild of Brig. Gen. William (Billy) Mitchell, whose goal was to demonstrate to Congress and the public the capabilities of the U.S. Army Air Service. For Mitchell, the Air Race was a first step in publicizing the capabilities and advantages of a well-equipped air fleet, able to defend the country in a future war.

The Air Race provided good casting: dashing pilots in their regulation leather helmets and jackets, riding breeches, knee high boots, and for some a silk scarf. They were colorful personalities to follow in the newspapers. Lt. Belvin Maynard, known as "the flying parson" because he left the pulpit to fly in the race, was accompanied by his dog, Trixie. Lt. Dan Gish, wounded in the war, checked himself out of Walter Reed Hospital in order to participate. On the first day his plane caught fire, but undaunted, he continued in a different plane. One lieutenant left at the halfway point to fly to his alma mater's football game. And a major was involved in a highly publicized argument over whether he or a lowly 2nd lieutenant had arrived in Long Island first.

The race takes its place in American aviation history, which began with balloons and gliders and reached an apex with the achievement of the Wright brothers in 1903. Before the U.S. entered WWI in 1917, courageous (or foolhardy) "barnstormers" began thrilling onlookers with their aerobatic displays, typically taking off from farmers' fields. Early barnstormers, sitting upright in front of the motor and exposed to the elements, took risks flying over Niagara Falls, buzzing the White House and flying upside down past the Washington Monument. There were so many fatal crashes that when the U.S. entered World War I, there were few original barnstormers still alive to join the U.S. Army Air Service. Nevertheless, the "sport" continued after WWI.

Planes were modified during the war. The practice of throwing bricks or grenades at an opponent in flight, for example, was replaced by stationary guns for both the pilot and the observer, whose seat faced in the opposite direction so he could train his rearward-firing guns at a pursuing enemy. The U.S. declared war in April 1917, but playing catch-up, the U.S. Army Air Service was not ready for combat until a year later. It was an American, the young, nattily dressed Brig. Gen. Mitchell, who hastened the war's end in November 1918 with his brilliant air strategy.

There was no easy transition to peacetime in 1919. It was a tumultuous year, and the Air Race in October was a welcome diversion for a nation unable to provide enough jobs for returning soldiers, racked by disastrous race riots, absorbed by a fear of Bolshevism on America's shores, and concerned by a multi-state steel strike. For those who sought alcohol to wash down their disappointments, there was frustration over the passage of Prohibition.

The Transcontinental Air Race, in addition to providing sensational headlines and entertainment for children who were let out of school to see an airplane for the first time, led to important safety improvements. The race demonstrated that many of the airfields were not safe, and exposed other problems, including aircraft defects, some of which could be rectified. It did not lead, however, to the immediate fulfillment of Brig. Gen. Mitchell's dream of an independent Air Force.

Due in part to the number of crashes and deaths during the Air Race, Congress was not forthcoming with financial support, and neither the government nor the public was interested in anticipating the idea of another war. Today, we can understand the resistance of the older military brass to an independent air force. They had been trained in the importance of the cavalry, and could not accept that airplanes could do a better job of reconnaissance, much less take an active role in defending the country or leading an attack on the enemy. Mitchell's personality got in the way of his message, culminating eventually in his court martial and conviction for insubordination in 1925. The U.S did not have an independent air force until 1947, 11 years after Mitchell's death. Its first Chief was an Air Race pilot, General Carl Spaatz.

LOST:

ONE AIRPLANE, TWO PILOTS

*T*HE GREAT TRANSCONTINENTAL Air Race of 1919 began simultaneously on October 8 from two coasts. Forty-four planes left Long Island on October 8 bound west for San Francisco, while 15 planes from San Francisco headed east toward Long Island. Most of the planes were American-made de Haviland-4s (DH-4s), two-seated biplanes that had seen service in WWI. Others included five captured German single-seated Fokkers and seven single-seated British fighters, the SE-5. The bicoastal event was headlined in newspapers all across the United States. Reporters found plenty to write about as planes crashed, pilots lost their way, and seven contestants died.

On the third day of the Air Race the telegraph operator in Chicago was among the first to transmit the dire message: "Plane #14 is missing." The plane had made the five required stops since leaving Long Island two days earlier and had been last seen in Bryan, Ohio, as it departed for Chicago on the afternoon of October 10. Before it left Bryan, the pilots were warned of dangerous weather, with fog and rain in Chicago, but chose to fly anyway.

The plane was a de Haviland-4 with two open cockpits and a Liberty engine, able to reach a speed of 128 mph. It carried no parachutes, no flares, and no way to communicate with the ground or fellow airmen in the sky. Pilots of DH-4s were warned not to fly in heavy rain, which could cause serious damage to the wooden propeller. After the second day of the race there had been five crashes involving four deaths. A missing plane was therefore of great concern.

The pilot of plane #14, Lt. Col. John N. Reynolds, and his copilot, my father, 1st Lt. Ralph B. (Baz) Bagby, were both veterans of the Air Service in France in WWI, winners of the Distinguished Service Cross and heroes of the war. Both believed that their experience flying in bad weather in France and Germany prepared them to fly to Chicago in spite of the fog and rain. During the war Reynolds had been commander of the 91st Observer Squadron of the U.S. Air Service, while Baz had flown 111 missions across enemy lines as an "observer" with both the French and the 88th Observer Squadron of the United States Air Service. Observer squadrons were particularly selected for attack by German aircraft because of the crucially important work they did. While the pilot maneuvered the craft over enemy territory, the observer carried out valuable reconnaissance, recording troop movements, taking photographs of the location of trenches, battery emplacements and airfields, as well as strafing the enemy on the ground with his Lewis machine gun and firing at the planes pursuing them.

By the time of the Air Race, Baz Bagby had acquired his pilot's rating, but he had only 57 hours of stick time. He more than made up for this meager piloting time with his precise mechanical and navigational skills and familiarity with the DH-4. His confidence and sense of humor were added assets. Each of these traits was needed as early as the second day of the race, when he and Reynolds experienced a forced landing in a farmer's field in Pennsylvania, resulting in broken landing gear and a damaged propeller. They eventually limped into Cleveland, exchanged the propeller for a new one and made some minor repairs, readying for their flight to Bryan, Ohio, the following day.

Baz and Reynolds rose at 4 a.m. on October 10 and prepared the plane for a 7 a.m. takeoff. They were hoping to fly from Cleveland to Bryan and on to Chicago and Nebraska. But the flight to Bryan took longer than expected, and at the Bryan airfield they were held up by a wire from Chicago saying not to proceed because the field was covered in water. Another wire announced a substitute landing field would be readied at Grant Park, a public park on the edge of Lake Michigan. The visibility in Chicago was reported to be poor, but as Baz later wrote, they were told to "come ahead if we wanted." Of course they wanted—they were in a race to win. Nonetheless, just half an hour after they left Bryan, the wind increased to a dangerous level for the small plane. Undeterred, they tried to maneuver around the storm, eventually heading north instead of west, but they couldn't escape it. Now, dangerously off course and headed in the wrong direction, they realized they had a choice: turn back or fly west over Lake Michigan to Chicago and make up for lost time. Even if the weather changed, the route over the water would be precarious, so they decided to turn back, find their originally intended route and fly into Chicago as planned from the south. On returning to their flight path, however, Baz wrote that they encountered "very low fog and another heavy rain." Over the small town of Buchanan, still on the Michigan side of Lake Michigan, they realized they couldn't make it to Chicago, and needed to descend for an emergency landing.

Baz, from his seat behind the pilot, had a better view of the ground than Reynolds, and directed him to a newly planted wheat field. As Reynolds came in for the landing he felt a slight rocking from side to side. Was it a shift in the wind? Were there problems with the rudder? He certainly didn't need any distractions. Both men were soaking wet in their open cockpits and exhausted from the strain of the last two days. Reynolds' hands ached from clenching the stick against the force of the wind. He would need all of his skills to land the plane if there was mud on the ground. They both knew the dangers of landing a DH-4 in the mud—the wheels, unable to roll, would stick like glue to the ground, causing the plane to nose over. The inadequately secured fuel tank just behind the pilot could break loose, crushing the pilot against the engine.

Leaning out of his open cockpit, trying to see through the mist and rain, Baz could see what Reynolds couldn't—the farmer's field awash in mud. The rocking continued, even stronger, putting the plane and both men in additional peril. Baz crawled out of his cockpit and worked his way back along the fuselage toward the rudder so that his body would act as a counterweight to the nose of the plane. This desperate maneuver had already caused the deaths of two airmen en route from San Francisco to Utah, and that same day would kill another in New York.

Why would men risk their lives to win this race?

HARPER'S WEEKLY

A JOURNAL OF CIVILIZATION

Vol. LIII   **New York, October 9, 1909**   No. 2755

A NEW KIND OF GULL IN NEW YORK HARBOR

AIR PIONEERS:

THE THRILL OF DANGER

*T*AKING DANGEROUS RISKS in the air did not begin with the 1919 Air Race. In the 18th century, balloonists were soaring to great heights in untethered multi-colored balloons. Benjamin Franklin, U.S. Minister to France in 1783, was an invited guest to witness the take-off of the first successful manned hydrogen balloon flight from the Bois de Boulogne on the outskirts of Paris. Ten years later President George Washington gave a signed "passport" to French balloonist Jean-Pierre-Francois Blanchard, who launched his balloon over Philadelphia in 1793. The passport instructed that wherever he landed he should be treated with "good will which may render honor to their country."[1] The balloon floated to a height of 5,000 feet, crossed the Delaware River and landed in Woodbury, New Jersey, less than 10 miles away. The flight lasted 46 minutes. The farmers were puzzled when handed the passport, but were impressed by Washington's signature.

The English Channel was crossed by a balloon in 1785, so in 1844 it seemed plausible that a balloon could cross the Atlantic. The *New York Sun* on April 13, 1844, carried a story that had been sold to the editors as a "first hand report." The headline screamed: "The Atlantic Crossed in Three Days." The account explained that the feat was accomplished by a large, elliptical silk balloon secretly designed and built in England to transport passengers across the English Channel. Inflated by 40,000 cubic feet of coal gas, it was steered by a three-foot rudder/stabilizer. Under the balloon was a four-foot-deep wicker basket for

FACING PAGE: **Wilbur Wright over the Hudson River, September, 1909. San Francisco Library.**

eight standing, passport-carrying passengers. Hanging above the basket were items to keep the passengers comfortable: "water casks, cloaks, carpetbags...a coffee warmer." The balloon lifted off from north Wales bound for Paris on a foggy morning in April and rose rapidly, but a strong wind blew pilot and passengers in the wrong direction, over the Atlantic. Having no other choice, they headed for America. The second day out the wind decreased and the balloon ascended to 25,000 feet. When the travellers eventually saw the coast of South Carolina, they descended. The writer exclaimed: "This is unquestionably the most stupendous, the most interesting, and the most important undertaking ever accomplished or even attempted by man."

Two days later the newspaper retracted the story. It had been a clever hoax perpetuated by a penurious Edgar Allen Poe. The editors covered their embarrassment by adding to the retraction, "We by no means think such a project impossible."

Nevertheless, balloons had a practical purpose as early as the French Revolutionary Wars, when tethered balloons were used for reconnaissance. During the Civil War both the North and the South used manned, tethered, gas-filled balloons for knowledge of troop placements. Above the range of artillery fire at 1,000 feet the crew could send messages by telegraph or signal flags to the commanders below. Balloons continued to play a part in reconnaissance on the frontlines in France during WWI.

The precursor to maneuverable manned flight was the semi-steerable glider. An early air pioneer, Otto Lilienthal of Germany, was the first to popularize and suggest the possibility of heavier-than-air flight. He constructed over 2,000 gliders of his own design, many with ingenious, fantastical, eye-catching wings, and guided their direction by moving his body. Neighbors and townsfolk watched him taking off from natural steep hillsides or from a 49-foot hill that he created. He died on one of his experimental flights in 1896.

Four years later, two determined and brilliant brothers, Wilbur and Orville Wright, tried their own luck to get a controlled glider to fly. From their bicycle repair shop in Dayton, Ohio, they had designed a speedy bike, but their heart was in creating a manned craft capable of flight. For their experiments, they would need wind for uplift, grass or sand for soft landing, and privacy, far from the prying eyes of those who might want to copy their ideas. They found the perfect spot at Kitty Hawk on the desolate Outer Banks of North Carolina, with its consistent winds, long stretches of sandy beach, and few residents. They spent the fall months there from 1900 to 1903.

Meanwhile, another designer, Samuel Langley, head of the Smithsonian Institution and a well-respected astronomer and physicist, was working on a catapult design for his tandem-winged Aerodrome, and prepared to launch it in October 1903. Patterned on a model he had built in the 1890s which had crashed in the Potomac River, Langley was nevertheless able to raise $50,000 from the U.S Army and a lesser amount from the Smithsonian, providing him the time and funds to have his design produced again. Launched with a catapult, which pulled rather than pushed the plane, it took off from a houseboat in the Potomac River and crashed in the river on its first flight in early October. After repairs, it crashed again in the river on December 8. Fortunately, his pilot survived. Finally, in 1915, the catapult design was successfully used by the U.S. Navy from a moving ship.[2]

On December 17, 1903, just nine days after Langley's Aerodrome fell in the Potomac the second time, the Wrights were ready to try a powered flight with an engine designed and built in their bike shop in Dayton. The plane was "whittled out of hickory sticks, gummed together with Arnstein's bicycle cement, [and] stretched with muslin they'd sewn on their sister's sewing machine in their own backyard on Hawthorn Street in Dayton, Ohio."[3] The winds were 20–25 miles an hour. Orville and Wilbur took turns lying on the lower wing as the craft flew, each staying airborne for seconds. The last and most successful flight of the day was flown by Wilbur and lasted just less than a minute. They were elated, and sent an enthusiastic wire home to Dayton. Unbelievably, little attention was paid to their success.

By 1905 Wilbur was flying, unannounced, around the 48-acre Huffman Prairie near his home, making the tour of 24-1/2 miles in 39 minutes. Passengers taking the *Springfield and Urbana* interurban elec-

Orville Wright's telegram of success to his father, December, 1903.

tric railroad would occasionally see the Wrights in flight from the train windows. Then the Wrights stopped flying in order to protect the details of their plane before it was patented or sold. They didn't fly again until 1908.

Meanwhile, Glenn Curtiss, a bemedaled bicycle and motorcycle racer from Hammondsport, New York, was also trying his hand at manned flight with his own engine and a new wing design. He was working with others, including Alexander Graham Bell. In contrast to the Wrights' secretiveness, Curtiss announced in 1908 that he would be flying a heavier-than-air flying machine, *June Bug*, on July 4th from a race track at Stony Brook Farm, just two miles outside of Hammondsport. Sponsored by the Aero Club of America, the event drew a crowd of 1,000 people who arrived by bicycle, motorcycle, and horse and buggy. Aeronautical experts and the press were on hand. The day dawned windy and wet, clearing by late afternoon. On his second try Curtiss, sitting in front of the engine clutching what looked like an upright bicycle wheel, kept *June Bug* aloft for one minute and 45.2 seconds, a paltry runner-up to the 39-minute unpublicized flight of the Wrights' machine three years earlier. Nevertheless, "pandemonium broke loose among the crowd." He received the *Scientific American* trophy for the first public flight in America. In 1908 Curtiss entered and won the First International Air Meet in France and began demonstrating his craft in front of awestruck crowds in France and the United States.

Once his patent was secured, Wilbur Wright, not to be outdone, followed suit by participating in air shows, setting records in distance and duration, and was celebrated in Europe and the U.S. by adoring throngs. His first public flight was in France on August 8, 1908, just a month after Curtiss's *June Bug* flight. By then the Wrights had acquired a patent for their design from the U.S. as well as several European countries and a signed contract with the U.S. Army and a French syndicate to sell Wright-designed planes. In 1908 the Wrights sold the Wright Flyer to the Army for $30,000. It was followed by a new design, the Wright Military Flyer, the following year, which was also purchased by the Army.

In 1909 both the Wrights and Curtiss were invited to participate in a 300-year celebration of the discovery of the Hudson River by Europeans. Curtiss declined on the day of the event because of the wind, but Wilbur Wright flew a round trip above the Hudson River between Governor's Island and Grant's Tomb and circled the Statue of Liberty in 33 minutes, a 20-minute flight today. The wary Wilbur had attached a 60-pound red canoe underneath the fuselage and carried a life preserver, just in case.

Both the Wrights and Curtiss created paid flying teams to perform at air shows and competitions. The more daring pilots began doing highly dangerous tricks. During a 10-day aviation carnival in Salt Lake City in April 1911, both teams were invited to participate in a race and to perform aerial maneuvers, including diving toward the ground and pulling up two feet from the field. However, a crowd of 12,000 was most thrilled when Curtiss flew his new invention, a seaplane. The Wrights discontinued their exhibition team that same year; six of their nine team members had perished in crashes.

In 1909 the Aéro Club de France issued Aviators Certificates to Glenn Curtiss and the

Glenn Curtiss sitting upright in his early plane. National Air and Space Museum, Smithsonian Institution.

Wrights. The Aero Club of America issued its first pilot licenses about the same time. Glenn Curtiss was the first on their list while the Wright Brothers received honorary licenses. It also issued pilot licenses for seaplanes and balloon and dirigible operators. The Wright Brothers set up a school in France to train pilots, followed by schools in Maryland for Army Signal Corps officers, a civilian school in Alabama, and eventually, the Wright Flying School in Dayton. Many of their students would fly in their exhibitions. Curtiss followed suit a year later with schools in Hammondsport, New York, and San Diego. Curtiss also offered to teach Army and Navy pilots for free.

In its early days, flying remained a sport with little sense of a practical application. As a sport it was particularly attractive to motorcycle riders, who found flying both faster and more dangerous than their land-bound bikes. The original seat of the early planes, as in the *June Bug*, was constructed so that the pilot was in front of the wings, clutching an upright steering wheel, fully exposed to the weather. At first, the challenge to the pilot was to fly higher or longer. Prizes were awarded, making each event a competition. In 1911, a 27-year-old motorcyclist, Weldon Cooke from Oakland, California, was the first to respond to a $1,000 prize offered by the Mill Valley and Mt. Tamalpais Scenic Railway Company to a pilot who would fly over the 3572-foot Mt. Tamalpais, north of San Francisco. The prize was later withdrawn because the flight was considered too dangerous. Undeterred, Cooke took up the challenge anyway. From the air over Berkeley, he dropped a letter to the President of the University of California, where he had been a student. This "air mail" letter was an early suggestion of a practical application of air flight. Cooke reached the summit of the mountain, but encountering wind and fog on the way to San Francisco, he changed his plans and descended 3,000 feet. Losing power, he slowly circled down to the village of Mill Valley and landed safely in a muddy area near what is today Sycamore Park.

Pilots who flew risky aerial demonstrations at county fairs or in farmers' unplanted fields came to be known as barnstormers. They were attracted by the financial awards, the thrill of danger, and the

adulation of the crowds. It is said that some of the crowd came to see
the fatal accidents which might occur as the pilots tried flying upside
down, doing loops, barrel rolls, and even walking on the wings. In 1913
Weldon Cooke died in such an event: flying on a vertical bank in a
canyon, he hit a downdraft and couldn't get his plane horizontal again—
just days after he had promised his mother he would give up flying.

The same year that Weldon Cooke responded to a $1,000 offer to
fly over Mt. Tamalpais, Calbraith (Cal) Rodgers, another aspiring aviator, found a $50,000 offer by William Randolph Hearst too irresistible
to ignore. Hearst's challenge was to fly across the country in 30 days –
the first transcontinental flight, an unheard-of proposition. Rodgers,
also an auto racer, had more flying experience than Cooke, including
flying lessons from Orville Wright. Rodgers was deaf but he didn't let
that inhibit his competitive spirit; he talked the Armour Meat Packing
Company into sponsoring him, agreeing to advertise their soft drink

**Lincoln Beachey racing Barney Oldfield, famous race car driver, in 1912. Library of Congress
Prints and Photographs Division (ID cph.3b18665).**

"Vin Fiz" on his plane's rudders and wings. And the plane? A specially designed Wright flyer, model EX, a biplane with two eight-foot pusher propellers (pusher propellers were behind the engine). His seat was located at the front just under the wings. Armour financed a three-car train that would follow Rodgers, containing a touring coach and a baggage car with parts that a specialized mechanic could use if there were any problems – and of course there were. Rodgers left Long Island on September 17 dressed in a business suit over sweaters, and travelled 104 miles to Middletown, New York, in two hours. His problems began the next day at take-off when he hit a tree and crashed into a chicken shed. It took three days to set his plane aright. Accidents unfortunately became the norm, with Rodgers experiencing broken bones and broken planes, but not a broken spirit. When it became obvious that he could not complete the trip in 30 days, he continued on, still following the train tracks (with a few mistaken detours on other lines) that would take him to the west coast. When he arrived in Pasadena there was a crowd of 20,000 to greet him, and 50,000 when he made it to the ocean at Long Beach after 84 days. (There was a month's delay between Pasadena and Long Beach after a serious crash in which both plane and pilot had to be repaired.) The plane had been mangled so many times that when he finished he only had "...one rudder and a single wing strut remaining from the original aircraft..."[4] This brave and determined man died four months later in a flying accident at Long Beach thought to have been caused by a flock of seagulls, one of which was found in the rudder of his wrecked plane.

On the west coast, another pilot had his eye on the Hearst prize. Robert G. "Bob" Fowler, flying a Wright Flyer Model B (the same as Rodgers), made his first attempt from Golden Gate Park in San Francisco and crashed 138 miles away in Colfax, CA. His second attempt from Los Angeles was successful but it took almost four months, so he too, missed out on the prize.

Women were also eager to display their aerial skills. Journalist Harriet Quimby was the first woman to receive a pilot's license in the U.S. She learned how to fly at Moisant School of Aviation on Long

WELDON B. COOKE'S AEROPLANE

Weldon Cooke's seaplane, 1913. Library of Congress Prints and Photographs Division (LC DIG-ggbain-13387).

Island in 1911. Other firsts in one year's time included Harriet being the first female to fly at night and the first woman to cross the English Channel. Described as "vivacious," "slim," and " beautiful," she wore a stylish purple satin flying outfit with knee high boots—certainly another first. She died in 1912 at a Boston Aviation event flying a French Blériot XI 1912 which crashed for no known reason. Katherine Stinson, the fourth licensed female pilot in America, was nicknamed "The Flying School Girl" because she looked like a teenager. Stinson was skilled at aerial feats such as the loop-the-loop. After being turned down by the Air Service in WWI because she was a woman, she nevertheless was determined to do her part in the war and became an ambulance driver for the Red Cross in France.

Barnstorming was even more popular in the 1920s, and women continued to participate. Bessie Coleman, of African American and American Indian heritage, grew up in a sharecropper's family in Texas, one of 13 children. In 1916, at age 23, she began working as a manicurist in the White Sox Barbershop in Chicago, where after the war she heard the firsthand stories of returning pilots. Inspired, she was determined to pursue a flying career. Although she was turned down by flying schools in America, she enrolled in Berlitz to learn French, and in 1920 left for

Barnstormer Lincoln Beachey over Niagara Falls, 1911. Library of Congress, Prints and Photographs Division (LC-USZ62-5840).

France, where she received her pilot's license. Back home, she soon realized that if she wanted to support herself it was best to become a barnstormer, so she returned to France and Germany for further instruction, came home and took up barnstorming, doing figure eights, loops and near-ground dips. She became a sensation, was billed as Queen Bess, and then died in 1926 when the Curtiss Jenny plane she was flying went into a dive, caused by a wrench caught in the engine of the plane.

In the 1920s some barnstormers were walking on wings from plane to plane, hanging on the wings and doing handstands on the wings. They made most of their money by charging for rides, but this entertainment lost its allure with the Depression. The most spectacular pre-war barnstormer, Lincoln J. Beachey, originally helped to design and fly dirigibles. On his first flight (1911) in a Curtiss plane, he found himself in a dangerous downward spin. Choosing a counterintuitive response, he pushed the stick forward and turned into the spin, which enabled him to survive to do that trick and many others for fame and financial rewards. That same year he flew 20 feet over Niagara Falls and under Honeymoon Bridge just above the rapids. He was the first to do figure eights and the vertical drop. In one stunt he raced a train and touched his wheels on the top of it. In another, repeated many times, he raced against Barney Oldfield, a well-known race car driver, as people placed bets on who would come in first. In a real race, Beachey would have won every time, but he and Oldfield worked out who would win, so that crowds kept returning to bet on the outcome. In 1914 Beachey buzzed the White House. President Wilson, looking up from his desk in the Oval Office, could clearly see Beachey heading straight for him before Beachey changed direction and flew upside down past the Washington Monument. Next was the Capitol, where people rushed out to the Capitol steps to see him. His awesome feats were described in newspapers, magazines, and newsreels, and he performed at the Panama Pacific International Exposition in San Francisco in 1915. There, sadly, at an aerial demonstration before 50,000, he attempted a dangerous maneuver in his new monoplane. The wings fell off and he fell to his death. Another stunt pilot, Art Smith, took his place at the exposition.

Barnstorming continued, almost as if each new participant looked for a crazier and more dangerous trick to entrance the crowd. In 1917 Lomer Lockyear first walked on a wing while he was in flight in order to screw a loose cap on a radiator. He then incorporated wing walking as part of his routine. Pilots were making money. They typically worked alone and usually charged $5 to take someone up in the air. They spent the night at a farmer's home "under a wing or in a hammock strung between the struts."[5] Some pilots did their exhibitions with a group known as an Air Circus, with an advance man who went ahead to advertise when the circus was coming to town. They charged higher prices for rides. In the 1920s some daredevil pilots were walking from plane to plane in flight and hanging from the wings. They were taking precautions, but the audience below couldn't see the harness or hooks strapped to their wrists. A member of a circus could average $1,500 per plane per day.

By the time Beachey died, WWI had already begun in Europe, and air power would play a key role in the conflict. Sadly, few barnstormers survived to join the U.S. Air Service when America finally entered the war in 1917.

➤ 3 ◄

WORLD WAR I:

DRAMATIC CHANGES

IN AIR POWER

*T*HREE YEARS AFTER Lincoln Beachey's death, my father, Baz Bagby, and pilot Louis (Bernie) Bernheimer, both first lieutenants, were on a reconnaissance flight in a two-seater British Salmsom 2A2 over the Meuse River in France, in territory held by the Germans. On October 30, 1918, their plane was accompanied by five French-made Spad fighters, so that Baz, the observer, could take photos with less fear of being shot down. But a dogfight occurred between the six American and nine German planes. Three German planes were shot down, one of them by Baz, before the Germans retreated. Baz wrote of the Germans: "I admire their good flying and their aggressive spirit...they are flying Fokkers, which are good at maneuvering, and fast driving busses [planes] but Bernie and I are working well together, and my two guns are natural shooters." He marveled that without "any words or signals, every time I'd swing my guns to the other side of the tail to shoot, Bernie'd swing the tail out of my way before I got the guns over all the way."

Well before the outbreak of WWI, European powers had been building up their stock of aircraft and other equipment in anticipation of a conflict. The U.S. did not follow suit, maintaining neutrality until April 1917, when Congress finally declared war. Consequently, America was unable to come to the immediate aid of its allies. When the war began in 1914 the 1st Aero Squadron of the U.S. Signal Corps had only 12 officers, 224 enlisted men and six planes. America had gained some experience in the air during a border war with Mexico in March 1916, but the planes flown, known as "Jennys," a Curtiss JN-3, did not perform well in strong winds or at high altitudes, and there were many accidents. The United States was abysmally unprepared for the kind of warfare occurring in Europe in which barbed wire and newly introduced tanks rendered cavalry useless, German submarines torpedoed neutral American merchant ships, German zeppelins bombed civilian London, and poison gas was used against both troops and civilians in Belgium in 1915.

In France, England and Germany, planes were being redesigned for use in an air war. When fighting first began, pilots had thrown bricks or hand grenades at each other, then progressed to using pistols. Eventually, pilot-controlled guns were synchronized with the rotation of the propellers. Cameras that could take panoramic oblique pictures (rather than just vertical shots) were added, and two guns were included at the rear of planes for the observer. There were no parachutes for the U.S. forces (the Germans were sympathetic to their use, but it was not universal) because those in charge didn't want planes abandoned by pilots when a crash seemed imminent. It was estimated that hundreds lost their lives as a result.

Before Congress declared war young American men, some already in France, volunteered for the ambulance corps (Ernest Hemingway served in France with the American Red Cross) and the French Air Service. In April 1916, a unit known as Lafayette Escadrille attracted 38 pilots who flew French fighter planes under the command of a French officer. The unit became famous because of their successes downing German planes. Those Americans who joined other French units came to be known, along with the escadrille, as the Lafayette Corps.

When Congress declared war in April 1917, America was divided between those who believed the United States should remain a country of peace and not be drawn into a European conflict, and those who wanted to support France and not tolerate either German bombing of American merchant ships or the sinking of the passenger liner *Lusitania*. President Wilson, a proponent of neutrality, changed his mind when he learned of a coded German telegram offering the states of New Mexico,

Arizona and Texas to the Mexican government if Mexico would support Germany! Wilson then had to move quickly to put the U.S. on a war footing and to get more of the public emotionally behind the war effort. At that time, there were only 131 officers, 1,087 enlisted men, 35 pilots and 51 student cadets in what was then an arm of the Signal Corps. An order increasing the manufacture of arms and planes was issued in June 1917. However, it wasn't until May 1918, a year after Congress declared war, that DH-4s with an American Liberty engine began arriving in France from the States. By then the Air branch of the Signal Corps had been replaced by the U.S. Air Service and Americans were trained in France by French observers and pilots in French planes.

Before the draft, Baz Bagby had graduated from the Massachusetts Institute of Technology. He responded to patriotic messages coming from Washington by leaving his first job at an armament manufacturing company, which automatically gave him a deferment, and by entering Officer Candidate School in Artillery at Fort Riley, Kansas. His joining the military was a surprise to his family. Although four of his brothers had gone to West Point or Annapolis, Baz had originally chosen a path having nothing to do with the world of war. He attended a small Missouri college, William Jewell, where he was on the football and track teams and captain of the baseball team. He graduated in three years and then took a year to check out possible future careers. He went to a tree nursery convention in Portland via San Francisco and played professional baseball as a catcher in the minor leagues, but finally chose to enter MIT, where he completed his mechanical engineering degree in two years.

My father's new decision to enter Officer Candidate School may have been influenced by President Wilson's propaganda machine, known as "The Committee of Public Information" and headed by journalist George Creel. Given a large budget, Creel doggedly worked overtime. Citizens were implored to create victory gardens and were inundated with patriotic messages in the form of newsreels, speeches by local leaders, songs, and colorful heroic posters by well-known artists. One, "I Want You" with Uncle Sam looking directly at the viewer and pointing his finger, became an iconic image of America and WWI. Another portrayed the Statue of Liberty garbed in the American flag with a Boy Scout at her feet. The posters were ubiquitous—plastered on billboards, barn walls, bus and train stations, in windows of homes, and smaller versions in magazines. The message was clear: Be a patriotic American; everyone (Uncle Sam, the Boy Scouts) expects you to do your duty. George M. Cohen's "Over There" was written the day after Congress declared war. The chorus, written to the tune of a bugle call, was an immediate hit.

Over there, over there,
Send the word, send the word over there,
That the Yanks are coming, the Yanks are coming,
The drums rum-tumming everywhere.
So prepare, say a prayer,
Send the word, send the word to beware,
We'll be over, we're coming over,
And we won't come back till it's over over there.

From April 13 to November 5, 1917, Baz was at Fort Riley. By the time he graduated as a second lieutenant he was eager to change from artillery to flying. He wrote home, "I think that is the branch of service that is going to be the biggest factor in winning the war...I'm not so fond of the artillery." However, he was turned down each time he applied to be a pilot, with the explanation that there was a greater need for observers than pilots. His one consolation was that as an observer he would at least be in the air. He probably hadn't heard yet that the German ace, the Red Baron (Baron Manfred von Richthofen) had told his pilots to "shoot the observer first."

After graduation from Officer Candidate School, Baz waited to be shipped overseas, and spent the next three months at three different Army camps in Texas, living in tents, taking care of horses (still thought to be essential to the military), receiving tactical instruction and playing football. Promoted to First Lieutenant, he finally boarded a troop train in February 1918 for the East Coast, still hoping that in France he would be trained as a pilot rather than as an observer. When the train reached New Jersey, Baz wrote that the locomotives were "blowing their whistles" in welcome, making them all proud to be an American serviceman. At the harbor, 84 American officers and 2,275 enlisted men packed themselves into the USS *Mercury*, a 526.4-foot-long, two-masted, two-funneled ship. Their 17-day crossing was agony for many of the seasick soldiers. Baz was sick for the first five days, incapable of keeping any food down. The ship smelled. Daily gun drills and abandon-ship drills helped to fill the time as they zigzagged across the Atlantic, praying that they would be able to stay out of the way of German submarines. Arriving in France on March 3, 1918, they landed at Bordeaux and were greeted by the YMCA, a welcome sight. The YMCA played an important role in the lives of every American soldier by providing hotels and activities for those on two-day or a week's leave in famous tourist destinations including, for some, the Riviera and Paris. Thanks to YMCA hospitality, Baz enjoyed future leaves in Paris, Versailles, Lyon, Cannes, and Nice. Now, setting foot in France for the first time, he was impressed that "at the hotel in port, Mrs. Vincent Astor was personally in charge of the dining room."

Baz immediately was charmed and amused by the French: "People go wild over Americans. Such a demo. In St. Louis it would mean that the Cards had won the pennant....To our soldiers it is just one grand big lark." The countryside is "so pretty I can't blame the French for fighting for it." At his first breakfast in a restaurant, the waitress "had a clean face and was pretty but what clothes! Woolen stockings and carpet slippers and one of Great Aunt Caroline's dresses." She not only overcharged them, but "did most of her talking with her shoulders." On the more sober side, he realized that in the villages there were no "French men or boys over 10, and females with contagious diseases had their hair bobbed."

During April and May 1918, Baz was impressed with the quality of observer training that he received from the French in aerial gunnery and photography. As a student, he was in the air and shooting every day from 6 to 10 a.m. and 4:30 to 8 p.m. His letters home were upbeat,

funny, and full of enthusiasm and optimism: "Ready to go! Americans will be far superior to the Germans."

Finally, in June, my father received his orders. He was the only American observer assigned to a French escadrille (a French Air Service unit)—"the best escadrille in the entire French army." He wrote that his work was like a "continuous vacation...peace would be very unwelcome." Now he could experience the value and necessity of an observer, particularly flying over enemy territory, locating German positions on the ground and passing that information to commanders in the field.

During five months (June 10 to November 10) Baz flew 111 missions, first with the French escadrille in French Spads and Breguets aircraft. In mid-July he was assigned to the 88th Aero Squadron, U.S. Air Service, where he flew in British Sopwith two-seaters for his first eight missions and for the rest of his time in Salmson 2A2s. Often poor weather, particularly fog, kept the men landbound, but when the weather cleared it was possible to do two missions a day.

While he was with the escadrille, Baz experienced a crash landing in which he and the pilot finished upside down. He described it to his family:

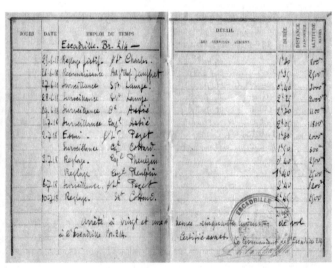

TOP: **Escadrille Br 214 log book, 1918.** BOTTOM: **Escadrille flights of Lt. Ralph (Baz) Bagby.**

American Lt. Baz Bagby and French Capt. Jean Charles exchange hats and jackets.

Capt. Floret of French Escadrille Br 214 and his Spad plane. Floret was the pilot of Baz's first flight with the escadrille; they crashed a few days later.

In the afternoon my capitaine took me up for what turned out to be a short ride. When we were at about 300 meters and climbing the motor suddenly lost its enthusiasm. We were too close to the ground to have very much choice about a landing ground except to dodge a railroad and small woods. We landed in a field of green wheat and when the wheels and lower wing hit the wheat we slowed down immediately and the Spad did the half loop, landing bottom side up in less than one second.

Luckily we were both strapped in so that we took the full trip and not a scratch. The plane did not fare so well losing the

Baz's drawing of accident in letter home.

propeller, part of the lower wing and damaging the tail. After he had asked me about 10 times in French and English and had assured himself that I wasn't hurt a particle, the capitaine said, "C'est la guerre Bagby, donnez moi une cigarette." Then he re-arranged his mustache.

When Baz was transferred to the U.S. Air Service 88th Observation Squadron, the escadrille had a boisterous and fun farewell dinner where Baz was "toasted in good French and bad English," and he in turn "toasted them in butchered French."

Originally the label "observer" had sounded passive to Baz, but at the front he quickly realized that his work was anything but. Besides reconnaissance and location of German troops and gunnery batteries, he acted as a gunner, bombardier, photographer, and liaison with allied artillery about where to place their fire. He was usually protected by fighter planes so that he could carry out mapping and photography. There was the added difficulty of communicating with the pilot, and some observers attached strings to pilots' arms to let the pilot know which direction he should take. With the frequent rain and fog in the summer and fall of 1917, pilots were forced to fly many missions at a low altitude, making them more vulnerable to the enemy artillery. Of all their duties, flying over actual combat doing "contact patrol" was the most dangerous, and when they returned, their planes would show the scars of artillery fire. After a mission, Baz would drop notes in a weighted bag to the Allied commanders below about what he had seen, and on his return would be cheered by the Allied soldiers in the trenches, "who threw everything they had up in the air."

Baz made fun of some of his other duties, such as dropping propaganda. "I seldom untie my bundles so that they drop very fast, and would knock a man cold if they hit him which is about the extent of their goodness. [German] Soldiers are more interested in getting food and sleep than they are in the mistakes of the Kaiser."

While flying with the 88th, Baz earned his first commendation, and was praised for his "coolness and devotion to duty [while he] brought

German plane over German-held France.

Lt. Baz Bagby (right) with pilot Lt. Fletcher McCordic after successfully downing a German Fokker.

down an enemy machine in the course of combat with 8 German pursuit aeroplanes."

While Baz was respected, praised, and given medals for downing a German plane, he noted with resignation that in spite of the observation work he did, which saved many lives, a downed enemy plane seemed more important. "Photos of the Boche [a derogatory French word for the Germans] back areas are more valuable than Boche planes shot down, but there is no credit [or] glory" attached to it. I have gotten more credit for simply downing a Boche than for all the rest of my work put together."

Baz wrote frequently of the fun he was having in combat. In his letters home he wrote not to worry, and kept sad news to himself, never expressing how he really felt when one of his companions had been killed during an air battle. However, the diary of Lt. Harvey Conover, a pilot with the 90th Observation Squadron, offers a glimpse into what many may have been thinking. In May 1918 Conover wrote that:

> as far as being killed is concerned, I can surely expect that everyone who stays in the game...gets his sooner or later, but all I ask for is a chasse plane [a pursuit plane] and I will be perfectly satisfied to play the losing game against fate and old man

Crashed German Fokker in Allied territory.

gravity....It is peculiar how we are becoming calloused to the deaths of our friends. Someone comes in and remarks casually that "so and so got his today....All of us, although we hope to get through, now realize how little chance we have. The very best airmen are getting killed daily...we can't help but realize how slight our chances are....We all think we will get it, but all persist in trying to find out when.

Again in September:

...it has now become so common that you accept the news of the death of a friend as you would the outcome of a baseball game. You say "oh is that so?" and straightway you forget it. You can't help wondering, however, when your turn will come.

The last section of Conover's diary gives a short bio of 23 men who have died, with warm comments about the fun they had together, and

Operations room of the 88th Observation Squadron. Pilots and observers check maps with observers' photos, planning next sortie. Lt. Baz Bagby fourth from right.

whether they were quiet or outgoing. In spite of his early comments about taking their deaths in stride, he apparently did care, and missed them. Most of these aviators died in accidents rather than in combat. He concludes with another list of 26 men who were missing or taken prisoner.

In October 1918, flying low to help troops being ambushed by steady artillery fire, Conover was "surprised by a crash" in which he suffered a serious loss of blood and extensive shrapnel injury to his leg. After enduring numerous ambulance rides over rocky terrain, and transfers to different field hospitals, he was finally put on a hospital ship that landed in New York harbor on December 9.

Baz was well aware of the differences between men serving in infantry and Air Service units. Men in the trenches were faced with mud, feces, rats, lice, and fallen companions. Their "reserve ration" included bacon or corned beef, hard bread or hardtack biscuits, packets of coffee, sugar, and salt plus a tobacco ration. On the other hand, pilots and observers had a dry bed to sleep in every night, a mess hall with fresh food (and in the escadrille, delicious food) and dry clothes. Furthermore, on short leaves airmen, distinguished by their insignia and swagger, received admiring looks.

Balloon companies were also part of the U.S. Air Service. Some men who signed up for the Air Service found (to their chagrin) that instead of flying planes they were put with a balloon company. It was a muddy business and dangerous but only one balloonist, Lt. Cleo J. Ross, died in combat. He was escaping his burning balloon when his parachute caught fire and he perished.

Baz referred in his letters to having to stay out of the way of allied "sausages" (yellow or gray observation balloons 90–200 feet long) while flying. It may be difficult today to appreciate the importance of balloons used by both sides during WWI. When stationed correctly they could provide key intelligence. The U.S. Air Service had 16 balloon companies (one to three commanding officers, five to 23 observers, and untold number of orderlies per company) operating in war zones beginning in March 1918. Personnel included 446 officers and 6,365 enlisted men. As the front line moved, balloon companies had to transport winches, gas bottles, anti-aircraft guns, telephone lines, and their large and clumsy deflated observation "towers" over muddy, potholed roads and abandoned trenches at night to a new and flat location, where they could be reinflated with hydrogen gas. Before the balloon left the ground two

Lt. Baz Bagby in flight gear, Germany, 1919.

observers crawled into their small wicker basket, 3 feet x 5 feet and 4 feet high, loaded with their equipment of binoculars, cameras, a telephone with wire to the ground, and a large board, which jutted over their basket with the map attached of the ground below. Sand bags and two parachutes for escape completed their equipment. Although balloon observers at least had parachutes, pilots didn't envy their work; it was both arduous and hazardous, and similar to the infantry in that they also slept in mud, ate cold food and had rats as companions. In one recorded case, rats ate the rubber of the balloon. The stress up in the air was keen: two observers spent "long hours suspended above the ground, often objects of shelling or aeroplane attacks, a lonely grueling experience. The strains it produced caused men to…develop nausea"[1]

ABOVE: A deflated balloon of the 2nd Balloon Company is transported to near the front line. The basket which could hold two men and supplies is on top of the balloon. LEFT: Balloon being inflated in the Argonne, 1918.

and there was always the fear of phosphine or mustard gas from the German troops below. Various assessments of a good observer included that they should have "no nerves," "beaucoup de sangfroid," and "be a little crazy."[2] Brig. Gen. Mitchell was impressed with the organization and professionalism of the balloon crew: "These men are the kind to have at the front."[3]

One balloonist described his ordeal:

From September 26 to November 11 we lived under the most trying conditions without any relief. Weeks passed when we were working and sleeping in mud six inches deep. During those days it was seldom

*that we were dry. Two French companies and one American
company were put out of action on account of sickness, but we
managed, probably through luck, to stick it out.*[4]

From March to November the balloon observers made 125 parachute
jumps, 122 due to enemy aircraft attacks and three by friendly fire. During this period 35 U.S. Army Air Service balloons were burned and 12
destroyed by artillery fire from the ground. Although the RFC (Royal
Flying Corps) of Great Britain honored their balloon observers with medals and commendations, the U.S. Air Service did not.

On November 2, 1918, Baz was returning from the latrine on the
88th Air Base when he overheard his superior officer talking to his staff
about how essential it was in the upcoming offensive to have information on the placement of enemy troops as well as the condition of bridges
held by the Germans over the Meuse River. He complained that the
weather was so bad that all planes had been grounded. Baz sought out
one of his favorite pilots, Bernie Bernheimer, with a proposition. Just a
month before, he and Bernie had flown over the Meuse, so it was familiar territory. Now they decided they would undertake a special mission
on their own. They flew through the fog, crossed into enemy territory,
and saw no other aircraft in the sky. Baz took the necessary photographs
of the bridges, strafed an airfield where "eight two-seater Halberstadts
were on the field in a position to take off...and started back, shooting
up two truck convoys, two batteries on the march, a bunch of wagons,...a
few automobiles and motorcycles until I had no ammunition left." This
was not the first time Bernie and Baz were the only plane to be out in
bad weather. The two had been reprimanded before for going out on
their own. This time, Capt. Kenneth Littauer, Chief of the Air Service
of the 3rd Army and commander of the 88th Observation Command,
said: "Bernheimer and Bagby at it again are they? Good work." They
both were awarded the Distinguished Service Cross. Among other honors during the war, my father also received the Croix de Guerre, Silver
Star, and commendations from the French, Belgium and U.S. Air Service. In the last week of the war on a strafing and bombing mission, Baz

dropped three 25-pound bombs by hand over the side of his plane.

The overall success of the last months of the war is attributed to the tactical skills of Brig. Gen. William (Billy) Mitchell of the U.S. Air Service for his organization and coordination of ground and air forces. He had begun his duties in the U.S. Army as a private during the Spanish-American War, moving up rapidly due to the influence of his father, a U.S. Senator. Just days before America declared war, Mitchell, then a major, had been sent on a

Lt. "Bernie" Bernheimer, pilot, 88th Observation Squadron.

fact-finding tour of France, where he met with Allied commanders and flew as a passenger over the front with a French pilot in a French plane. He became the most knowledgeable American in aviation in Europe, was promoted to Lt. Colonel in May, and Colonel in August. According to Air Force historian Walter J. Boyne, Mitchell lost a competition with Brig. Gen. Benjamin D. Foulis to become Chief of Air Service, American Expeditionary Force, and was made instead Chief of Air Force, First Army—"the top combat position." Mitchell's winning strategies in the last air battles of the war were exemplified by the St. Mihiel Offensive in September 1918. In that battle, he commanded the largest air armada ever assembled—almost 1,500 aircraft consisting of American, British and French units that devastated the German front and shortened the war. He chose Maj. John N. Reynolds as Group Commander of the Army Observation Group. Mitchell's decision to elevate observation units over pursuit and bombardment was, according to Boyne, "true in all armies during WWI...aerial observation was crucial for the successful conduct of the artillery and infantry operations."[5] However, communication between ground and air was difficult. Airmen ingeniously used "radios, light, sound of fire [from their] machine guns and weighted message bags"[6] to pass essential information to artillery, while on the ground the troops relied on flares, coded cloth, and even handkerchiefs to get the attention of the airmen. Mitchell was promoted to Brigadier General and received numerous medals, including the Distinguished Service Cross, for his brilliant and successful plans. Months later he would become the "father" of the 1919 Transcontinental Air Race, placing his hopes for the future of American air power in his plan for the race. Baz spoke of Mitchell with great admiration, and was proud to write home that he had participated in all five major Allied attacks organized by Billy Mitchell.

No discussion of WWI should ignore the services of the cavalry, an essential feature of earlier wars. While the border skirmish with the paramilitary forces under the revolutionary Pancho Villa of Mexico

Fellow airman helps observer lift camera into observer's cockpit. Signal Corps 22389.

during March 1916–February 1917 provided experience for American pilots in their Jennys, it also was useful for cavalry units. At the time, most of the military assumed that any future conflict would also rely heavily on cavalry for reconnaissance and for dramatic charges against the enemy. Before entering the war the U.S. supplied thousands of horses to England for use on the front line, at the same time maintaining 15 regiments of U.S. Cavalry. When the U.S. declared war, the number of cavalry regiments was immediately increased, and images of horses were displayed on recruitment posters to entice men to enlist. The U.S. sent close to a million horses overseas; the total of horses used at both East and Western fronts was a staggering six million.[7]

However, the reality of trench warfare exposed the dangers to both men and horses. Horses developed skin disorders and their manure caused health problems for the soldiers. They were killed by enemy artillery (7,000 in one day at the Battle of Verdun in 1916), and disposal of their bodies was difficult. The use of barbed wire and the introduction of tanks dramatically reduced the need for cavalry, so that many of these units were converted to the artillery.

Still, cavalry continued to play an important role during WWI, particularly in the muddy conditions at the front. Horses pulled ambulances and carried supplies and ordnance. They were also active in the last offenses against the enemy: the cavalry, acting as scouts, participated in the St. Mihiel offensive in September 1918, riding five miles into German-held territory at night.

At the conclusion of the war the U.S. Air Service had destroyed 756 enemy aircraft and 76 balloons, while losing 289 planes in battle and 48 balloons. The Air Service personnel included 7,726 officers and 70,769 enlisted men.

World War I was among the deadliest conflicts in history. Military and civilian casualties totaled over 38 million. For the U.S. there were 53,402 combat deaths (with even more non-combat deaths) and 204,000 wounded out of a population in 1918 of 92 million. In 2010 the U.S. Department of Defense released a new study of the number of U.S. WWI casualties: 116,526 deaths, and out of these, 106,378 occurred with those

Baz (in cockpit) with the other 88th observers who were competing during the Occupation for best photographs of ravaged France and abandoned German hangers.

serving in the U.S. Army (including the Air Service). In Europe, a whole generation of young men lost their lives. It was a costly victory.

The U.S. was battling other forces as well. Influenza and pneumonia killed more American soldiers and sailors during the war than did enemy weapons. The flu pandemic, known as the Spanish flu, affected American soldiers at home and in France. It is thought to have begun in an Army camp in Kansas and spread as the soldiers were moved from camp to camp. Further exposure occurred on troop ships and in the trenches. At Baz's home in Missouri his adored little sister, Jean, died of it in 1916 at the age of four. In France, his friend Bernie Bernheimer was hospitalized with flu, putting an end to their many hours of flying together. Bernie survived, but the Spanish flu is estimated to have caused 50 million deaths worldwide.

While waiting for the official ending of the war, and the signing of the Treaty of Versailles, the Allies occupied the German Rhineland. Baz served eight months in Germany in 1918 as a member of the Army of Occupation. It was a police action, and those in the Air Service had few duties. Baz managed and played on a baseball team—"never played better"—and taught classes in Artillery School—"a lot of unnecessary drill." To maintain their skills, pilots of the 88th flew with observers who competed in photographing the countryside, including battle sites with trenches, ravaged villages, and hangars still containing German planes. Baz won a silver cigarette case for his photographs. Best of all, he learned how to fly. His training was with friends skimming over Germany, Luxembourg, and the former front lines in France. He earned his pilot's rating in April 1918 flying a Salmson 2A2.

On March 1, a popular pilot, Fletcher L. McCordic, known affectionately in the 88th Observation Squadron as "the General" or "the Gen" for his quiet, assured manner, died in a crash in a German Fokker that he was testing. Baz had flown with him in combat and picked up the tricks of the flying trade from him during the Occupation. Baz was a pallbearer at the outdoor funeral. He wrote McCordic's parents describing what a brave, generous, and humble man their son was, and how he had protected him in combat from German fighters intent on shooting down the plane with the observer.[8] True to form, my father did not mention the tragedy to his own parents. His oldest son, my brother John, remembered as a young boy going with his father to visit

McCordic's parents in Winnetka, north of Chicago, years after their son's death.

Baz had told his family he would leave military life after the war, but the joys of flying over "beautiful Luxembourg," Paris at 50 meters, and landing at Orly, caused him to doubt his decision. His log reveals the thrills and hazards of his 32 solo flights. In addition to having fun doing spirals, figure 8s and slips, he was brutally honest about what went wrong—usually a problem with landings, and breaking an axle. In early May his log includes "tried a few slips...broke left axle... stalled on landing...spiraled and 200 m slip." On May 13, he made two landings without the motor after executing "a few figure eights and a spiral down from 1000' in 4 turns." On May 28, he "chevalled" (rocked sideways?) in landing and tore a wheel off the axle. He broke two more axles during landings on June 14 and June 19. It was a relief to his family to read about his last flight in Europe on July 8. They did not know that he had decided to remain in the military if he could stay in the Air Service.

The end of the war and return home of American troops was not without serious practical concerns. What would the U.S. do with so many trained pilots and observers and with airplanes outfitted for war? How would the returning soldiers, aviators, and sailors be received? And what about the more than 300,000 African Americans who had served in the war? When the draft was announced in June 1917, more blacks had been drafted proportionally than whites in the South. African Americans who served in France were mainly employed in con-

Lt. Fletcher McCordic's funeral, 1919.

struction work, digging trenches and unloading supplies at the docks, but they also served in two segregated combat units. A separate Officer Training School was created for them in Des Moines, Iowa; however, after the first graduation class the school was discontinued. African American soldiers and officers in France faced disgraceful bullying and belittling acts: many white soldiers refused to salute a black officer, and white officers even lied about black successes on the battlefield. Yet the African American experience in the Army in France was better than what they had become accustomed to in the States. They returned home with a new determination to achieve parity. Everyone who had served in France had been changed forever.

Baz's mother, Lilian Armstrong Bagby, knitting woolen "helmets" for aviators with Baz's youngest sibling, Sarah, 1919.

➤ 4 ◄

1 9 1 9 :

HOPES, ASPIRATIONS,

REALITY

*T*HE TROOPS RETURNED HOME on crowded ships from December 1918 through July 1919. Some of them were returning with the scars of war: lost limbs and "shell shock." Most of them were eager to get out of the service, reunite with their families, take up their civilian lives and return to normalcy. But what was normal in 1919? It was a year that tested the assumptions of our moral values with nasty incidents of racism, immigrant baiting and strike-breaking. Yet the year also included the finalization of women's suffrage and eye-catching distractions of spectacular American skills, such as a military transcontinental motor convoy and air races.

In February 1919, Brig. Gen. Billy Mitchell sailed from Liverpool on the troop ship *Aquitania,* a large four-funneled ship capable of handling 7,460 passengers. It didn't take long before Mitchell, dressed smartly in his belted tailored jacket, riding breeches, and polished boots, assumed control by reviewing the troops with his staff for two hours every day, on every deck, preceded by a bugle corps made up of African American soldiers. It was the ship captain's only experience of a highly disciplined troop ship, and he was impressed and grateful. Mitchell also gave impassioned lectures to the officers, which included illustrations of the air war in France, and stressed the importance of maintaining and increasing the strength of the Air Service in preparation for a future war. These ideas, it must be said, conflicted with President Woodrow Wilson's ideals of "peace without victory" and a "war to end all wars."

Baz's 10-day ocean voyage home that July from Brest was on the smaller two-masted, two-funneled ship, USS *Zeppelin*. Capt. Harry Truman, Commander of an artillery brigade during the war, had left France on this same ship in April.

My father returned to the States during a tumultuous summer in America. Fortunately, he was able to have a relaxing month's leave in his Missouri hometown of New Haven before reporting to his first assignment at Langley Air Field, Virginia, in September. While he was in France, he had expected any day to run into his brother, Maj. Carroll Bagby who was in artillery. ("After all, France is no bigger than Missouri.") But the war concluded before his brother made it to Europe. During the war Baz's frequent letters home kept the family up to date. He found time to write to Johnny, his 10-year-old brother, to mind his mother, and responded to his sisters' requests for money, keeping the amount in his logbook. Seventeen-year-old Helen had written for advice about how she could get to France, and Baz suggested she apply to the YWCA, so that she could help the YMCA, which was active in France. Helen never made it overseas, but Baz's family found other ways to help: his mother knit warm caps for men in the Air Service to wear underneath their regulation leather helmets, and his sisters knit sweaters for men in the trenches.

During his home leave, Baz had time for socializing, fishing in Boeuf Creek, helping at the family tree nursery, playing baseball and tennis, riding horseback and hunting. In the warmth of the family Baz delighted in singing "The Dixie Kid" as he spelled out the words on the toes of his youngest sister, Sarah, age one-and-a-half, the last of his 11 siblings. His sisters tried to pick out on the piano the latest ragtime tune of "Somebody Stole My Gal" and showed him the "one step" that was danced to it. There were long dinners around the family table, reminiscing about childhood baths in the kitchen, their trip to the 1904 World's Fair in St. Louis and returning on the midnight train, and the annual family picnic in May for their parents' wedding anniversary.

Baz was a born storyteller, and he entertained his large family and friends with the more humorous aspects of his life in France and Ger-

many. He explained a photo [see p. 23] he had sent home to Helen while
he was still with the French Escadrille. Baz and his French pilot, Jean
Charles, had exchanged hats and jackets and fooled a visiting higher-
ranked French officer who walked into the mess. The officer asked a
question of the "French" pilot, who, not understanding the French idiom
about food, mumbled an "avec plaisir," followed immediately by the
"American" observer with the correct response in impeccably accented
French. The puzzled officer took a long hard look at the mustached
"American," another look at the clean-shaven "Frenchman," raised his
shoulders in a Gallic shrug, and left. The two guffawed, and quickly
changed back into their own jackets and hats before there were any re-
percussions.

The Bagby family had their own stories to tell, some of them serious, and some full of gossip of the town and relatives. Many momen-
tous events had happened in America while Baz was with the Army of
Occupation in Germany. His sisters proudly told him about the moral
victory of gaining the right to vote. In June, shortly before their brother's
return, there was a Joint Resolution of Congress for women's suffrage.
One of the objecting senators from Mississippi had tried to add a rider
that it was only for white women, but his rider was defeated 62–19,
and the Resolution finally went to the individual states for ratifica-
tion. The climate had changed from just six years earlier, when a *New
York Times* editorial tried to shame its male readers who were supporting suffrage by telling them to "act like men."

Baz was familiar with the Prohibition amendment discussed endlessly during his time in Europe. Ratified in January, America had suc-
cumbed to the plea of mothers and children to protect their families
from the evil of drink, memorialized in the 19th century song, "Father, dear father, come home with me now." Baz wondered if it would
last. He was amused by the current song "Sahara—we'll soon be as dry
as you." He was not averse to Prohibition, having written home from
France that, "The American custom is to get drunk, but not so for the
French." In France, it is "just a sociable hour or so over the newspaper
and latest gossip...prohibition is just as necessary or rather just as ad-

visable in America as it is impossible in France. I'm glad that the states are to be bone dry." On the other hand, he eventually agreed it should be repealed, since it was targeting the poor with arrests and home invasions, and ignoring the well-to-do and politicians who could always find top grade alcohol when they wanted it, and whose homes were not visited by law enforcement.

Baz and his family talked about the amazing stunts of pilots participating in "Flying Circus" events. These highly popular Air Service events, organized to raise money for U.S. war debts, covered 45 states across the country and typically lasted just one day. In most cities people had never seen a plane in flight, and farmers and ranchers drove over 100 miles to see the show. Children were let out of school for the day, and many businesses were asked to close from 1 to 4 p.m. so that all could see the skill of American, French, and Italian pilots. The highlight of the day was a mock battle between pilots flying German Fokkers against other Air Service pilots in American Curtiss Jennys. The "dogfight" was interrupted when American pilots flew into the battle in Spads and SE 5's, and with many spins, turns and nosedives on both

Air Service Newsletter, May 29, 1919.

sides, chased the Fokkers away. In the Midwest alone, the Flying Circus performed in 25 cities. Baz's family was not able to attend the show in St. Louis on April 14, or in Kansas City on April 30, but now, with their brother at home, they could listen with rapt attention about his experience in actual air battles with Fokkers flown by authentic Germans.

His family told him that the disastrous race riots, which had begun in East St. Louis when Baz was in Officer Training in 1917, were continuing. The cause of the conflict was complex. An influx of African Americans from the rural South to urban centers in the East and Middle West had begun in 1916. This first exodus lasted until 1930. Known as the "Great Migration," one and a half million men, women, and children fled to New York, Cleveland, Pittsburg, Detroit, Chicago and St. Louis in hopes of escaping Jim Crow laws and yearning for racial, social, and economic equality. The situation was exacerbated when they were joined by other blacks, also intent on equality, just back from the war in France.

Of greatest concern to most of the returning doughboys was finding a paying job. Even in October 1917, during the war, Lt. Harvey Conover was worrying about his future life in his diary: "What will I be satisfied with *après la guerre* providing I get through. My present mode of life, the experience I have had and the knowledge I have gained from travel and association, will have rendered me unsuitable for the humdrum existence I will be fitted for. Never will I be satisfied to settle down to such a life, and I look upon the future with some uneasiness." This very thought was expressed in "How Ya Gonna Keep 'Em Down on the Farm?," a popular song introduced in early 1919, suggesting that many soldiers who had left farms to fight in the War would not want to return to rural America:

> *They'll never want to see a rake or plow,*
> *And who the deuce can parlez-vous a cow?*
> *And how ya gonna keep 'em down on the farm*
> *After they've seen Paree?*

Demobilization (December 1918–July 1919) spewed out thousands of young men, black and white, to compete with each other for scarce employment, and when they weren't successful, they looked to scapegoats for their troubles. After the Russian Revolution, a fear of Bolshevism was insidiously linked with African American men. Even President Wilson was concerned about the attraction and told someone in private that "...the American Negro returning from abroad would be our greatest medium in conveying bolshevism to America."[1] Linking blacks to Bolshevism made them an easy target for the unemployed, restless, returning soldiers. Race riots begun in America during the war intensified. From May 10 to October 1 there were 34 race riots, a lynching, and approximately 241 deaths (of which 207 were African American men, women, and children). Ironically, this four-and-a half-month period came to be known as the "Red Summer."

Riots were not limited to southern states. They occurred as well in Connecticut, Pennsylvania, New York, and in Chicago, East St. Louis and Omaha. Some of the immediate triggers for violence included rumors of rape or murder of white women. An African American youngster swimming off a "white" Chicago beach was stoned until he drowned.

The rhetoric was paranoid and outrageous. According to Eric Freedman, Professor of Law at Hofstra University, a proposal for a union of sharecroppers in Arkansas was attacked "in a massive race riot" because a committee of local leaders claimed the union was a "deliberately planned insurrection...established for the purpose of banding Negroes together for the killing of white people."[2] The Justice Department ignored the findings of its own agents, who discovered that there was no evidence of conspiracy by the sharecroppers. Baz's family, horrified by the increase in lynchings (from 36 in 1917 to 76 in 1919) were hopeful that a fellow Missourian, the Republican Congresssman Leonidas Dyer, would have success with his Anti-Lynching Bill submitted to Congress in 1918. It passed the U.S. House of Representatives in 1922, but never made it out of the Senate because of a filibuster by Southern Democrats.

At the same time as the race riots, America was being distracted

by a more positive event—
a motor convoy across the
United States. When Baz
returned home the Trans-
continental Truck Con-
voy was already under-
way, and his family was
tracing its route on a map
in their sunroom. Baz told
them how the Old Guard
reluctantly gave up their
reliance on cavalry and
grudgingly accepted the

Newly constructed bridge for trucks in motor convoy. July–September 1919. Eisenhower Presidential Library and Museum.

value of planes and trucks. The motorized wagon, first bought by the
Army in 1907, was a key to the success at the Front, moving men and
supplies to new areas. By the time America went to war, the Army and
Navy had purchased over 90,000 trucks.

After the war, the War Department, responding to pressure from
the Good Roads Movement and the Lincoln Highway Association,
agreed to put together a truck convoy from Washington D.C. to San
Francisco, a trip that lasted from July 7 to September 6. The goal of the
original sponsors was the improvement of road conditions on the yet-
to-be completed Lincoln Highway from Washington D.C. to San Francisco. Sixteen years earlier, a car had been driven across the continent,
but no trucks had successfully made the trip. The War Department
had a different goal: to test how efficiently trucks could cross the country with soldiers and supplies in the event of a future war. They wanted
the soldiers conveying the trucks to act as if the United States had
been attacked by an Asian enemy, and to move as quickly as possible.
However, they hadn't anticipated that the convoy would be slowed to
a standstill by enthusiastic crowds.

The parade of 80 trucks and military vehicles included support vehicles such as a medical/dental unit, two mobile machine shops, a black-
smith shop, two spare parts stores, a searchlight, four kitchen trailers,

and two motorcycles, which went ahead to report on the conditions of the road. Over three million people are estimated to have viewed the convoy as it moved across the continent. Everywhere, in big cities and small rural communities, local dignitaries took advantage of the event with speeches and parades, followed by the press and newsreels.

Heading west, the convoy moved on paved roads until it hit Illinois, where it was slowed by uneven dirt roads, which grew muddy after rain. Obstacles continued with sand in Nebraska and dirt through the desert. California with its numerous paved roads proved to be the exception. Where bridges were missing, new ones were constructed. Eighty-eight wooden bridges collapsed under the heavy vehicles and had to be rebuilt. Over the course of the trip there were accidents aplenty but no fatalities.

Lt. Col. Dwight D. Eisenhower, an official observer at age 28, was one of 35 officers who accompanied 258 enlisted men on the 62-day journey. Thirty-seven years later, his experience with the motor convoy helped convince President Eisenhower to support the Federal-Aid Highway Act, authorizing a system of interstate and defense highways.

Before the motor convoy left the East Coast, another area of unrest erupted in America. There was increasing discontent on the part of American steel workers. The cooperation between employees and management, so vital in wartime, began to crumble further after the war, when steel companies did not keep promises of raised wages and improved working conditions. The companies tried to curtail the influence of the American Federation of Labor by denying permits for meetings, arresting union organizers at train stations, and denying work to men with large families. Miners in Pennsylvania went on strike in April, and an industry-wide strike was called for September. The massive steel strike attracted 350,000 demonstrating workers and closed down one half of the steel industry. The intensity of the protest surprised industry executives with its numbers of discontented workers and broad representation of mines and steel mills from eastern and middle western states to as far west as Pueblo, Colorado. On October 6, two days before the Transcontinental Air Race began in Long Island and San Francisco,

President Wilson called in the Army to control strikers in Gary, Indiana. The majority of the steel workers were unskilled employees from Southern and Eastern Europe demanding better working conditions and a role in the governing of the mill. For their efforts, they were clubbed, arrested, jailed and fined, no match against the powerful U.S. Steel Corporation, which outmaneuvered them by banning mass demonstrations, calling in strikebreakers from Mexico, infiltrating the unions, and announcing that the workers were "agitating Communists." The president of an aerial transportation company arranged to have former U.S. Army Air Service pilots and observers keep track of strikers from the air. They flew in two-hour relays within Pennsylvania and Ohio. Newspapers picked up the Red Scare theme and soon the workers lost in the court of public opinion. The strike was broken by January.

Just as the Truck Convoy was nearing San Francisco and the steel strike was taking an ominous turn, planes returned to the news. The simultaneous round-trip air race between Long Island and Toronto on August 25–26, 1919, was sponsored by the American Flying Club of New York and the Aero Club of Canada. Maj. Gen. Charles Menoher, Director of the U.S. Air Service, assisted the American Flying Club at the field stops in Buffalo, Syracuse, and Albany. There were both civilian and military entries with an array of 12 different types of planes, including the newly designed Curtiss Oriole. Due to heavy wind, rain, and hail, only 28 out of 52 entries finished the round trip. The winner for speed was Lt. Belvin Maynard from North Carolina. A former WWI pilot, he flew a DH-4 in the Air Race with an average speed of 133 mph.

Two balloon distance races took place in Missouri, in early September. The first, between the U.S. Army and the Navy, involved six balloons and was won by the Army, even though the winning balloon landed in Lake Michigan and was rescued by a passing boat. The second, in October, was hosted by the Missouri Aeronautical Society. Ten balloons competed. The winning balloon made it to Dunbar, Quebec, a distance of 1,050 miles. Baz missed observing these races. Just before Labor Day, 1919, he said goodbye to his family and left Missouri for Langley Field, Virginia.

As if the year 1919 had not already brought enough angst to the country, professional baseball, that most American of sports, showed its ugly face that fall. The Chicago White Sox, the expected winners of

the 1919 World Series, were pitted against the Cincinnati Reds. In the first inning of the first game, Eddie Cicotte, the White Sox star pitcher, hit the Reds' lead-off batter, second baseman Morrie Rath, in the back. Other "errors" followed. It wasn't

Curtiss planes lined up at Roosevelt (Mineola) Field for Long Island/Toronto Air Race. National Archives Photographs 342-FH-3B 7270.

long before sports enthusiasts began talking about a possible fix by some on the White Sox team. A year later it was determined that the outfielder and star of the team, "Shoeless Joe" Jackson, plus seven teammates, had indeed thrown the 1919 World Series for money. The hitting of Rath was the signal that the fix was on. This became known as the Black Sox Scandal. A reporter wrote that an incredulous young boy, seeing Jackson after his grand jury testimony, asked him, "It ain't true, is it, Joe?"[3] For my father the suspicion of unsportsmanlike behavior in his favorite sport was disappointing, but not surprising. According to Baz, the owner of the White Sox was widely disliked for underpaying his players and for neglecting to have their uniforms cleaned regularly in order to save money. Soon Baz was saying with humor, "Say it ain't so, Joe," in regard to Prohibition, local Chicago politics, and eventually, the behavior of his four children.

Reflecting on his family's accounts of what had happened during 1919, Baz saw the year as a series of tragedies and moral conflict counterbalanced by distracting extravaganzas and a few victories—all overlaid by his family's blanket of good will, optimistic spirit, and love.

At Langley Field, Baz's log records his first flight in the U.S on September 5, as a passenger with pilot John Reynolds, now a Lt. Colonel,

Lt. Baz Bagby (left) with his DH-4 at Langley Field, September, 1919, before the Air Race.

in a DH-4. They soon found they had much in common. Both had participated in the last five air battles in France in WWI led by Brig. Gen.
Mitchell, Baz as an observer in the 88th Observation Squadron, while
Reynolds was Commander of the 91st Observation Squadron, and later
head of the First Army Observation Group. Baz began flying solo at
Langley in the DH-4, and familiarized himself with its mechanical
advantages and its shortcomings. Little did either pilot dream that a
month later they would be flying as a pair in a transcontinental air race
in the DH-4. And never could they imagine the sensation that race
would cause.

The Transcontinental Air Race, scheduled for October, would dwarf
the Long Island–Toronto race in number of pilots and planes, types of
planes, number of field stops, and duration. Newspapers across the
country gave it front-page press. On October 5, three days before it
began, the Sunday edition of the *New York Tribune* headlined the event
as the "Greatest Aerial Race in History."

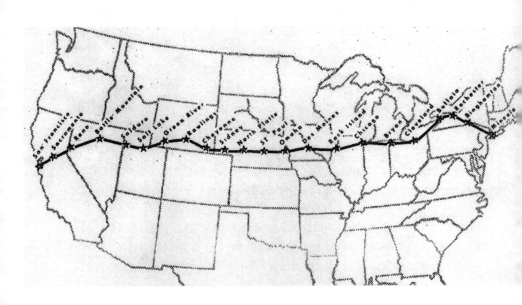

Control Stops of the Transcontinental Reliability and Endurance Test.

FROM LEFT: San Francisco, CA; Sacramento, CA; Reno, NV; Battle Mountain, NV; Salduro, UT; Salt Lake City, UT; Green River, WY; Rawlings, WY; Cheyenne, WY; Sidney, NB; North Platte, NB; St. Paul, NB; Omaha, NB; Des Moines, IA; Rock Island, IL; Chicago, IL; Bryan, OH; Cleveland, OH; Buffalo, NY; Rochester, NY; Binghamton, NY; Mineola, NY. (Long Island). Mineola Field was renamed Roosevelt Field after the death of pilot Quentin Roosevelt, son of Theodore Roosevelt, who died in combat in WWI, July 1918. From R.L. Bowers, "The Transcontinental Reliability Test."

5

PLANS FOR AN AIR RACE:
A GAMBIT FOR RECOGNITION

*T*HE TRANSCONTINENTAL Air Race was Brig. Gen. William Mitchell's brainchild, born of a desire to promote the value of air power in future wars and to gain attention and support for an independent branch of the Air Service, distinct from the Army and Navy. Mitchell believed that another war was inevitable, and that air power would be dominant in winning that war. He hoped that the hoopla of an air race would advertise the virtues of air power and impress the public with its reliability and its potential practical applications.

When Mitchell returned to the United States in February 1919 as a popular WWI hero, he assumed he would be appointed Chief of Army Aviation. Instead, he was placed under Maj. Gen. Charles Menoher, who served in France as the Commander of the 42nd Infantry Division, VI Corps. Mitchell became Menoher's G-3 officer, an assistant chief of staff in charge of training and operations. Despite the fact that Menoher would now be Director of the U.S. Air Service, his experience was with artillery, not air. Clearly, the two men would not see eye to eye.

Nevertheless, Mitchell didn't waste any time before promoting his ideas. Friends in Congress had introduced legislation to support an independent air command, but it didn't yet have the support of powerful political and military figures, including President Woodrow Wilson, Secretary of War Newton D. Baker, and Assistant Secretary of the Navy Franklin D. Roosevelt. There was not much time to convince these key players before the upcoming hearings in Congress. Mitchell hoped a dramatic race in the air would carry the day for his goals.

The Air Race was not Mitchell's only headline-grabbing adventure. To demonstrate the breadth of air power and its advantage over a naval fleet in future wars, he planned (and eventually carried out) a staged bombing of captured German warships in Chesapeake Bay.

In Washington, Mitchell, in his tailor-designed uniforms, was a dashing figure. He was a horseman, bon vivant, and giver of parties. His wealthy father, a U.S. senator from Wisconsin, gave him access to politicians who might support his ideas. As a child, Mitchell had moved easily with men of stature and high rank, and was allowed to sit at the dinner table with guests of his father. He didn't hesitate to participate in the conversations. As an adult, his ease within a ranked society such as the Army was often annoying to his superiors. Mitchell's supporters in the Air Service saw him as a passionate visionary. His detractors in the infantry, Navy, and Congress came to view him as arrogant, proud, and presumptuous.

Mitchell was an inspiration to Baz Bagby and John Reynolds, who wanted to participate in his schemes for publicizing the importance of the Air Service. The Air Race appealed to many former WWI pilots who, in peacetime, had lost their focus and missed the glamour and excitement of war. The race would provide them with another challenge in which their flying skills could be recognized, and they looked forward to competing with other pilots. The Eastern airmen originating in Long Island, New York, and the Western airmen starting from San Francisco would not be part of a team. Those flying solo, as well as those who were flying with a passenger, would be competing as individuals within their own East or West group.

The race was not going to be as easy as it originally seemed to the World War I veterans. They were on their own. Each landing was at an unknown field; the various altitudes at the landing fields demanded different strategies in taking off and landing. They were not returning to the same billet. They had to locate fuel and replacement parts themselves, and if they crashed, there were no squadron members, planes, or ambulances looking for them.

The race was given the official title "Transcontinental Reliability and Endurance Test" to lend it a serious sounding rationale, but the pilots wrote and spoke of it as a race, as did the press. On September 18, the chief of the National Weather Bureau was consulted; he reported that the best weather for the race would be the first three weeks in October. Alerting existing airfields and building new ones for landings en route could not be completed by October 1, so October 8 was chosen for the start, an unfortunate decision, because a spate of terrible weather east of the Mississippi blew in on October 9.

Lt. Col. Harold E. Hartney, an associate of Mitchell's, laid out a one-way course hopping across the United States, with 21 required control stops. The average distance between control stops was 123 miles. The plan was later changed to make it a round-trip race. The route avoided the Appalachian Mountains, but included the Rockies and the Sierra. Between Omaha and San Francisco, pilots would be able to follow railroad tracks, referred to as the "iron compass," but otherwise they were on their own with only postal maps, which lacked mountain ranges and elevations.

Supporting the racing aspect, different categories were established for winning: "elapsed time" (crossing the conti-

Brig. Gen. William (Billy) Mitchell in front of his DH-4 Bluebird. Photograph by A.E. Toepfer.

nent in the shortest total time, with no credit given for those assigned a late start time) and "speed" (shortest actual flying time, disregarding all time spent on the ground for bad weather and emergency landings, and allowing for a late start time). There was also an "endurance" category for never having to change motors, and a "handicap" category based on the type of aircraft. Ultimately, however, newspaper reporters ignored the different categories and acknowledged as winner the first pilot who landed on the opposite side of the continent, not appreciating different departure times or terrible weather conditions that grounded some pilots for hours, even days.

The Air Race was open to military pilots recommended by their commanding officers. All were required to alight at each control stop for at least 30 minutes, but could remain for 48 hours, if they chose. The commanding officer at each control stop was to show the pilot the location of the next landing field to the east and west. Flying time was calculated from the time the wheels of the plane left the ground at one control stop to when they hit the ground at the next. Any emergency landing in between control stops was included in the flying time. A detailed list of necessary supplies was to be delivered to each control stop before the race. Stopwatches and chronometers were recommended for accurate timekeeping. Pilots were required to circle the field before landing in order to be aware of wind and ground conditions. Anyone who disobeyed would be disqualified. There was to be no flying on Sunday.

Some control stops were already functioning as airfields, but others had to be created or enlarged. Nearby communities were asked to provide cleared and leveled air fields 2,500 feet long, although many of the existing fields were only 1,200–2,000 feet long. All those contacted responded positively, but as the race proceeded, it was clear that airfields with barbed wire and ditches presented life-threatening problems. One field in Green River, Wyoming, was too close to a canyon and had to be eliminated as too dangerous. Another field, in Chicago, flooded.

The three-page instructions to control stop commanders before the race included public relations requirements as well. They were to contact the mayor, Chamber of Commerce, Red Cross, YMCA, and Knights of Columbus to explain the seriousness of the "Reliability Race" and to impress upon them that their cooperation would help them to "establish the prestige of their town" as well as gain future unnamed benefits.

Control stop commanders were expected to have sufficient gasoline and oil for some 60 planes, be aware of local conditions, know the location of nearby emergency landing fields, have maps for the adjacent control stops, and arrange for telephone or telegraph communications. If a plane was known to have left the previous control stop and was late, the commander was to fire Very pistols (flare guns), and form a large "T" with lit gasoline so that the pilot could spot it from the air and also have an idea of the wind direction.

The planes in the race all had open cockpits of various designs. The overwhelming majority of the planes were DH-4s, a two-seater biplane designed in Great Britain and manufactured in the U.S. with an American Liberty engine. Other planes included German Fokkers with Mercedes Benz engines; Britain's two-seater Bristol fighters and single-seater SE-5s (Scout Experimental 5s), noted for speed and maneuverability; French Le Pères and a Spad; Italian SVA; American Martin Bombers carrying three passengers; and a Thomas Morse single-seater.

During the race, the pilots' ranks ranged from 2nd Lieutenant to Brigadier General, and the passengers were either officer pilots or mechanics, most with a rank of Sergeant. A speaking tube was used for communication between the two men. In the DH-4, communication was handicapped by the fuel tank located between them.

The DH-4 was popularly known as the "flying coffin" or "flaming coffin" because if the plane tipped forward at landing, particularly in mud, the fuel tank could slide forward and kill the pilot. A few DH-4s in the Air Race, known as "Bluebirds," had been remodeled, with the pilot's cockpit behind the fuel tank instead of in front of it, thus eliminating this danger. However, problems with its Liberty engine stopping in flight also contributed to the DH-4's deadly reputation.

THE MAIN PLAYERS FROM LONG ISLAND

In the days before the Air Race began, the predicted winners included **Lt. Belvin Maynard,** a young divinity student known as "the flying parson," piloting a DH-4. He had been a test pilot in Tours, France, during WWI, and in February 1919, earned the world's looping record of 318 consecutive loops in 66 minutes. Six months later he won the air race between Long Island and Toronto. Maynard's passenger in the Air Race would be **Sgt. Wm. E. Kline,** who had been a mechanic before he entered the Air Service. During WWI, he also served in Tours with the AEF Training Center for 21 months.

Another early favorite was **Lt. Col. Harold Evans Hartney**, flying solo in a captured German Fokker. A Canadian barrister and musician, Hartney graduated from the University of Toronto and the University of Saskatchewan. He played cornet in a town band and trumpet in the 49th Highlanders. Hartney had originally served in WWI in Canada's Royal Flying Corps, but was seriously injured when shot down by the "Red Baron" in February 1917. After his recuperation, he transferred to the U.S. Air Service and commanded the 27th Aero Squadron. He downed at least five German aircraft, making him an "ace." He also received a Distinguished Service Cross. Hartney had a unique advantage in the race, as he had laid out the course.

The only professional athlete in the race was **1st Lt. Baz Bagby** who had played baseball in the minor leagues the summer before he went to M.I T. At William Jewell College Baz was a member of the unconventional Hobo Club, which required members to have hitched train rides illegally in boxcars 500 miles, and have the ability "to get something for nothing." 1st Lt. Baz Bagby was one of 14 Air Race participants to have seen combat during WWI, and one of eight who had been awarded the Distinguished Service Cross (DSC) for their valor in the war.

Partnering with him in the DH-4 was **Lt. Col. John Reynolds.** In 1916, he had flown with the 1st Aero Squadron in the border skirmish against the Mexican revolutionary, Pancho Villa. During WWI, Major Reynolds was Commander of the 91st Observation Squadron and was beloved by the men who served under him. They referred to him affectionately as "Major John" rather than the appropriate title "Major Reynolds." When he first took over command, the pilots had complained that they were not being assigned as solo fighter pilots, and would be flying with an observer. He won them over by explaining that observation work was key to success in the war, and that the pilots would also have a machine gun to down German planes. A skilled pilot and leader of men, Reynolds received two DSCs.

Competition among the airmen was fierce, as each could lay claim to considerable skill and courage. **2nd Lt. Alexander Pearson** enrolled at the University of Oregon but left to join the U.S. Army when America entered the war, later transferring to the Air Service. He was an Army test pilot and served as a scout for the Transcontinental Motor Convoy of 1919. During the Air Race, his aviation skills would be tested and admired.

Son of a general, **Capt. John Owen Donaldson** was no stranger to courage when he entered the Air Race. As a student, he left Cornell to join the Royal Flying Corps in Canada. When America declared war, he switched to the U.S Air Service. On September 1, 1918, Donaldson was shot down in France and captured. He escaped the next day with another prisoner, tried to steal a German two-seater to fly out, was wounded in the back by a sentry, yet managed to escape. A week later he was caught again while swimming in a stream, and three days later escaped once again and made his way to safety in Holland. A WWI Flying Ace with seven victories, he also received a DSC.

Perhaps the flyer with the least potential for finishing the Air Race was **1st Lt. Daniel Gish,** a former race car driver who until recently had been a patient at Walter Reed Hospital in Bethesda, Maryland, recovering from World War I injuries. During the war, he was a member of the 1st Night Pursuit group, known as the Suicide Club, because flying at night with no instruments, in a British single-seat Sopwith Camel, was highly dangerous. In August 1919, he was a contestant in the Long Island-Toronto Air Race. A photo in Washington's *Evening Star* before the race shows a handsome young pilot in the cockpit and an exotic woman (an Egyptian "princess") standing next to the plane with the headline: PRINCESS SAYS GOODBYE TO WOUNDED PILOT BEFORE AIR RACE. Unfortunately, bad weather forced Gish to return to base. On the day before the Transcontinental Air Race, the *Brooklyn Daily Eagle* reported that Gish and Capt. Guy de la Vergne, French air attaché, flying to Long Island from Baltimore, "fell at Baltimore but got another machine and came on in it." An omen, perhaps, of the many challenges Gish would face during the Air Race.

THE MAIN PLAYERS FROM SAN FRANCISCO

Capt. Lowell Smith was considered to have a good chance of winning the race. He had been a mine worker near Battle Mountain, Nevada, and a race car driver before he became an aviator. While John Reynolds flew against Pancho Villa in 1916, Smith was on the opposite side flying *for* Villa. He switched sides in 1917 and joined the U.S. Army Air Service. His "lack of higher education" was apparently a drawback until local authorities and his Congressman went to bat for him.[1] He went to work to improve his educational credentials and graduated from San Fernando College and the Military School of Aeronautics at the University of California, qualifying as a pilot in October 1917. He was commissioned as a first lieutenant in December 1917, and promoted to captain in October 1918. Three months before the Air Race Smith set a non-stop speed record flying in a DH-4 Bluebird from San Francisco to San Diego, a trip of 610, miles in 246-1/2 minutes.

Looking to the future, the only airman in the Transcontinental Air Race who would become a full general in WWII was **Maj. Carl "Tooey" Spatz**. He had graduated 97th out of 107 students in his graduating class from West Point. He acquired his nickname at West Point from a fellow student, F.J. Toohey, who also had red hair. Spatz (pronounced "spots") flew with the U.S. Army Signal Corps in the war with Mexico and with the Air Service in WWI. During just three weeks in France, he managed to shoot down three enemy planes, received a DSC, and was promoted to Major. Spatz was a leader in the Flying Circus aerial demonstrations in 1919.

During the race **2nd Lt. Emil Kiel** and Major Spatz were close and testy competitors. Kiel graduated from Stout Institute in Menomonie, Wisconsin, and from the Primary Flying School at Kelly Field, Texas, in March 1919. He later became a flying instructor for the 91st Squadron at Mather Field in Sacramento, the squadron that Lt. Col. Reynolds commanded in France.

Every one of the participants, arriving from all across the United States, was eager to show his prowess. They began to gather, some as early as three days before the race, at Roosevelt Field (formerly Mineola) in Long Island and at the Presidio Field in San Francisco. Newspaper articles helped to dramatize the race and kept it newsworthy, usually on the front page. On October 5, three days before the race began, a reporter for the *New York Tribune* described it as the "most ambitious ever undertaken."

There was much to entice readers. One pilot, John B. Wright, arriving in Long Island, found there was no plane for him, so he assembled the necessary parts and entered the race in plane #42. Another entrant, Lt. Hiram W. Sheridan, had wowed crowds a month earlier at the Police Field Games with his parachute jumps. He flew in the race in plane #40. Tragically, two pilots making their way to Roosevelt Field to participate were felled by hazy or foggy skies. Maj. Patrick Frissell died when his plane turned over on landing, and Col. Townsend F. Dodd was killed when he crashed into a tree. Dodd had enjoyed a distinguished aviation career: the first commissioned U.S. Army aviator, he was the sole recipient of the Mackay Trophy for best airman of 1914 and a receiver of the Distinguished Service Cross during WWI. At the time of the fatal accident, he was commandant of Langley Field and had recommended both Reynolds and Bagby for the race. Typical of my father, he did not share this tragic loss, or any other bad news, in his letters home.

The day before the Air Race the front page of the afternoon edition of the *Brooklyn Daily Eagle* (28 pages, 3 cents) announced that the race was "the blue ribbon event in flying history." The reporter described

Fatal crash of Lt. Col. Townsend Dodd on way to Roosevelt Field for Transcontinental Air Race. National Archives Photographs 342-FH-3B 7282.

Roosevelt Field and the "brilliant sunshine of a perfect flight day...filled with the droning of motors and white wings of a fleet aloft. Pilots were trying out their machines, putting them through their paces or tuning up for the supreme event."

On October 7, there was an inspection of the planes by the authorities at Roosevelt Field. Maynard was in trouble. He wrote later that he was "severely reprimanded" for fitting his plane with non-regulation material as he had done in the New York-Toronto Race, which "added about ten miles an hour to its speed."[2] Apparently he had used wire that would have helped him increase his speed. He complied with the rules and was allowed to fly.[3]

On the other side of the continent, the *San Francisco Chronicle* also described the pre-race takeoffs and landings that were happening in front of a crowd of officers and civilians at the Presidio Field, a strait at the edge of San Francisco Bay. (Construction of the Golden Gate Bridge would not begin for another 14 years.) However, these were not exercises to inspire confidence. As was true of the Eastern group, most of the planes were DH- 4s with their ill-placed gas tank, not counting the three modified and safer "Bluebird" design. Pilots complained that Presidio Field was dangerous because of its small size and unfavorable winds. On October 7, pilots had to land with the wind, and three of them flying unmodified DH-4s had near-fatal accidents. Lt. Edward Wales overshot the field and landed in a hay-filled ditch. Maj. D.H. Crissy, fighting the wind, may have made an unintended ground loop at landing, and Lt. E.C. Kiel made four attempts at landing, all while his passenger, Sgt. F. McKee, who had climbed out of the cockpit to help weigh it down, was clinging to the rear of the plane "for dear life."[4] This may have made for great theater, but it was a disturbing portent of things to come.

It was clear from the onset that there would be serious problems ahead, among them the design of the DH-4, insufficient planning for finding missing planes, and lack of visible lights in the Midwest and West to help guide pilots to the landing fields. Contrary to the balmy predictions for October, there were gale winds, heavy rain, and snowstorms, turning flying fields to mud and damaging propellers and wings. The weather became a dangerous enemy.

There were other problems, many of which could have been avoided. Pilots and their observers had difficulty locating the control stops on the maps provided. They lacked information about the terrain at the airfields. Communication between control commanders was through telephone and telegraph, but there was no air-to-ground communication between the airmen and the control commander, not even radio. Some of the control stops were not prepared for emergencies, and they ran out of fuel. Tragically, many pilots had no training or experience in flying over mountains or landing at high altitudes. The men had trouble resting at night because they couldn't get the noise in the open cockpit out of their heads even when they tried to sleep. Too frequently driving rain, snow, clouds and fog obscured the land below and sometimes, spurred on by a fierce determination to win, pilots made life-threatening and foolhardy decisions when flying in these dangerous conditions. Just as in the war, there were no parachutes. And to top it off, when fire occurred, airplanes made of wood and canvas were quickly destroyed.

The unsung heroes of the Air Race would turn out to be the farm-

In the Path of the First Transcontinental Air Derby

(Copyright, 1919, New York Tribune Inc.)

A DH-4 surprises farmer, wife, and two children, and frightens pigs, chickens, cows, and horses pulling cart, which spills its contents. Cartoon by Ding Darling. *New York Tribune,* **October 14, 1919.**

ers and ranchers who helped downed airmen in corn and wheat fields, fed weary pilots, put them up for the night, located fuel, provided transportation for damaged plane parts, and in one case, guided a lost pilot to a safe landing with the aid of a flashlight.

TRIUMPHS AND TRAGEDIES

DAY 1: EASTERN AIRMEN

*T*HE AIR RACE BEGAN on October 8 at Roosevelt Field, Long Island. The weather was clear, with little wind (17 mph), but it was chilly. Visitors wore fur coats or heavy wraps, bonfires were built to keep the mechanics and guards warm, and aviators looked "like football players" with sweaters over their regulation flying outfit of riding breeches, knee high boots, leather jackets, leather helmets, and goggles. The Ladies of the War Camp Community Service passed around sandwiches and coffee. A band played. The festive atmosphere was enhanced by dignitaries including General Mitchell and Assistant Secretary of War, Benedict Crowell. There were the inevitable speeches, which the pilots, for the most part, ignored. They were busy checking on their planes, chatting among themselves, and greeting friends they hadn't seen since the war and Occupation. They heard the band in the distance, and those leaving later in the day observed General Mitchell doing aerial stunts in an SE-5.

The first plane to depart, piloted by Lt. J.B. Machle, left at 9:10 and circled the field. The race was on! Lt. Col. Hartney was next at 9:13. Many wondered if his plane, #11, a captured Fokker, would outdo the less flashy DH-4s, the most prevalent plane in the race. Lt. Belvin Maynard was the ninth to leave in his DH-4 with "Hello Frisco" written on the side. Many of the other pilots, eager to best the winner of the Long Island-Toronto race, groaned when his plane, #31, was given an early departure time, putting him hours ahead of others, such as Lt. Col. John Reynolds and Lt. Baz Bagby in plane #14, who were assigned an afternoon departure. As Maynard taxied to the starting line, his German police dog, Trixie, broke loose from Maynard's wife and headed for his master's plane. Maynard scooped him up and handed him over his shoulder to the rear cockpit, where his mechanic, Sgt. W.E. Kline, suddenly became a transcontinental dog sitter. This quick, spontaneous action brought laughter and endeared Maynard to the press. He didn't bother circling the field and headed straight for Binghamton, New York.

Another break with military protocol occurred when two young women, sisters, ran out of the crowd to Lt. D.B. Gish's DH-4 as it was about to leave. The girls gave the fliers gifts, and one of them, standing on tiptoe, gave the surprised pilot and his copilot, the French air attaché, de la Vergne, a kiss. Were they aware of Gish's history? Did they know he had been a very recent patient at Walter Reed hospital, still recovering from a WWI night raid crash? He had checked himself out so that he could "visit his family in Seattle." When asked if he wanted transportation he said, "No. I'm going by airplane."[1] He then left to participate in the Long Island-Toronto Air race in August, and here he was again for the transcontinental competition, wearing a steel brace in each leg.

There was another surprise in the planned activities when Assistant Secretary Crowell told Gen. Mitchell that he would like to go up, too. A plane and willing pilot were found, and Crowell was equipped with a flying jacket and helmet. But the pilot, Capt. M.G. Cleary, was able to keep the plane airborne for only seconds before the engine sputtered and the plane fell on its right wing and turned over. Mitchell and the crowd watched in horror and then relief as they saw the two men emerge from the wreckage. Crowell, although "visibly shaken quipped that it was the shortest flight on record."[2] The takeoffs continued.

Departure times were determined by the number on each plane: odd numbered planes were to leave first. This arrangement was skewed by chance or design to favor the higher-ranked pilots as well as Maynard, the predicted winner. As the race progressed, it was clear that the earlier departure time had conferred important privileges, such as less waiting time at the control stops for fuel and greater press coverage highlighting the first arrivals at each airfield. Baz wrote home later that they were "very unlucky" in their departure time.

His plane was the 26th to depart, three hours after Maynard. At the starting gate, aviator Maj. William Schauffler gave Baz and Reynolds the good luck insignia of his WWI observation squadron in France—a pair of dice, one for each. They would need it. They made good flying times: Binghamton in one hour, 30 minutes (1:30), Rochester (1:05), and Buffalo (0:40.) However, at the first two control stops there were so many planes ahead of them that they had to wait for gas, and by the time they reached Buffalo the control stop commander, who had misunderstood his orders, would not let any of the 18 planes there continue after 4 p.m. Concerned about wind, each plane was tied down with ropes and stakes. Baz wrote that originally he had believed they "would have made it easily to Cleveland before sundown." However, with time now to check their plane, they realized that "the propeller was out of line, and the vibration had caused a leak in a soldered joint in the radiator." Thus, the control stop commander's decision probably helped them avoid a crash. Fortunately, they were able to get a ride into Buffalo to have the radiator repaired and also to pick up another propeller, the first of many in their race across the continent. The repairs, finished at 1:30 a.m., gave them only three-and-a-half hours of sleep before they had to ready the plane for an early takeoff for Cleveland.

Maynard and the other morning departure pilots out of Long Island were not held up at Buffalo. By dusk Maynard, a true competitor, was ahead of everyone, the only pilot to reach Chicago that first day. He wasn't expected. The *Chicago Tribune* had predicted no one could make Chicago on the first day. He had landed at each of the seven control stops, made sure that he didn't stay a second longer than the required 30 minutes, and had flown 810 miles, with a total flying time of six hours and 45 minutes. When he and Sgt. Kline arrived at the Chicago control stop, the confident Maynard told a *Tribune* reporter, "I'm tired...It was a long hard grind but we're going to win this race." He then turned down a room in the city, preferring to spend the night at the field in the rustic quarters of the Aero Club so that he would be ready for takeoff at first dawn. It was an uncomfortable decision, as he wrote later: "Our mattresses were stuffed with hay and our pillows filled with straw. We were dug out of bed in the middle of the night by the cameramen for the Chicago papers."[3] The photo that appeared the next day did indeed show a very tired looking pilot.

In contrast to Maynard's good fortune, mishaps on that first day for the rest of the Eastern flyers included four wrecked planes, three in New York and one in Pennsylvania. Gish's plane caught fire over western New York, yet he somehow managed to land it, and both he and his copilot, Capt. de la Vergne, escaped uninjured. De la Vergne lauded Gish's skill in landing a plane in flames and gave him a trophy that he had won during the war. Gish, instead of dropping out of the race as did others whose planes had crashed, returned to Long Island for another plane. The mishaps and recoveries of this one lieutenant are a study of courage and self-reliance difficult to match. De La Vergne also had nerves of steel, continuing in the race as a passenger in a Martin Bomber.

The first fatal accident of the Air Race was a crash in Deposit, New York, that killed the mechanic, Sgt. W.H. Nevitt. The DH-4 piloted by Col. Gerald Brant suffered an oil line break. The engine failed and the plane plunged to the ground, killing Nevitt and injuring Brant.

By the first night, the Eastern flyers were spread along control stops from Rochester to Buffalo, where John Reynolds and Baz Bagby were trying to sleep; to Cleveland, where Hartney was one of four resting pilots; to Bryan, Ohio, where the two pilots closest behind Maynard slept; and to Chicago, where Maynard, mechanic Kline, and Trixie were sleeping near the leader's plane.

DAY 1: WESTERN AIRMEN

In contrast to the pleasant weather on Long Island, the first day for those flying from San Francisco to New York began at 6:30 a.m. with a high fog. At this early hour, there were about 200 visitors at Presidio Field, compared to the 2,000 at Roosevelt Field. The differences didn't stop there: only 16 planes were in the competition from San Francisco compared to the 44 that left Long Island, and instead of flying over the

Major Dana Crissy at Presidio Field before the race, Oct 7, 1919. Crissy is at far right; his mechanic, Sgt. First Class V. Thomas is at far left. Third from left is Lt. Wm. Goldsborough; fifth from left is Lt. E.V. Wales. Courtesy Golden Gate National Recreation Area, Park Archives (GOGA 34007-09).

flat landscape of New York and the Midwest, the route involved climbing over the hazardous Sierra Nevada and Rockies. Most of these Western pilots were familiar with mountains and high altitude flying, though not necessarily with the actual airfields. The unfamiliar mountains would eventually bring difficulties and even death to the Easterners.

A lottery decided which plane would take off first. Fourteen planes left San Francisco in just 15 minutes, finally escaping the fog when they reached 3,000 feet. The 15th plane was delayed by engine malfunction, and the 16th did not make it to San Francisco from San Diego in time to start the race.

Maj. John Bartholf left San Francisco, flying solo in an SE-5. He wrote that the most difficult and treacherous part of the trip to Long Island was the first day, "flying on your nerve" with no place to make an emergency landing over the Sierra Nevada mountain range. First there was a "dense blanket of fog in the morning" followed after Sacramento by a steep "climb, climb, climb with a wide open throttle and no possibility of [making an emergency] landing. There is nothing like 100 miles of Sierra Nevada mountain peaks—with the possibility of being driven down by engine trouble, snow, fog, rain or a rip in the fabric—to keep you alert."[4]

Maj. Carl Spatz took off before 2nd Lt. E.C. Kiel, but Kiel reached Sacramento first. At their seventh and final stop of the day, Buena

Vista Field in Salt Lake City, Captain Lowell Smith arrived first, followed by Spatz and Kiel. This triumvirate would battle for first and second position all across the continent to New York.

Montage of Western flyers at Buena Vista field. 1. DH-4; 2. SE-5; 3. Lt. R.S. Worthington; 4. Capt. Lowell Smith; 5. Lt. J.G. Hall; 6. Master Electrician F.D. Moon; 7. Maj. C. Spatz. *Salt Lake Tribune*, Oct. 9, 1919.

Eventually, 11 planes flew the 618 miles over the Sierra Nevada mountains, arriving in Salt Lake before sunset. One of these was so damaged at landing that it couldn't continue in the race. Another flight ended in tragedy. Maj. D.H. Crissy, the commander at Mather Air Base (after whom the Presidio Field was later named), and his mechanic, Sgt. Virgil Thomas, were killed when their plane spun out of control during a high-altitude landing at Buena Vista Field. Crissy was blamed as being inexperienced with the DH-4, yet Lt. Alexander Pearson (one of the Long Island flyers), who was not there, gave a more complex account in an interview two weeks later with the *New York Tribune*. Pearson reported that just before Crissy tried to land, Thomas climbed out of the cockpit and was riding the tail in order to help Crissy by putting weight over the tail.

However, Crissy aborted the approach and climbed again. Now, the weight of Thomas on the tail "upset the balance of the machine and it went into a spin 200' from the ground" and crashed in two to three feet of muddy water.[5] According to a different account years later, Thomas was standing in his seat waving to the crowd below, and Crissy side-slipped inadvertently, plunging into three feet of stagnant water. "Hundreds of spectators ran into the water to help and found the aviators in the twisted wreckage. Holding the heads of the pilots above water to prevent them from drowning, it was five minutes before emergency personnel could cut through the wire."[6] That was too late.

Crissy and Thomas were the second and third deaths in the race, and it was only the first day. The *Salt Lake Tribune* described a second crash in which a "catastophe [was] averted admirably by a skilled pilot who "made the best landing" of all the western pilots arriving that day from San Franscisco. At landing, Lt. S. Hall's plane hit a bank in the field and "sailing from the ground [made] a high leap with its running gear broken and dangling. The crowd held its breath...as it descended again...its nose plowed into another embankment." Besides the broken propeller, a wing was broken off and the radiator and crank were smashed. Lt. Hall was disappointed to have to leave the race." Gen. Mitchell's supporters could be forgiven for harboring doubts that the race would serve as positive publicity for the reliability of air travel and the necessity of a separate air command.

DAY 2: EASTERN AIRMEN

On October 9, the frontrunner, Belvin Maynard, left Chicago's Ashburn Field at daylight heading west, well ahead of the other Eastern flyers. He hoped to make another seven stops that would put him in Cheyenne, Wyoming, by the end of the day. Those airmen closest behind him arrived in Chicago later in the morning and faced a dangerous field: an overnight rain had turned the marshy landing area into a muddy quagmire. Two planes had nosed over in thick mud, destroying their propellers. One pilot, unable to locate the control stop, landed in a baseball field in Washington Park over eight miles away. A haystack was quickly set afire to help guide other pilots in the right direction.

Eighteen planes, along with John Reynolds' and Baz Bagby's, spent their first night at Buffalo, far behind Maynard, and left at 7 a.m. the next morning for Cleveland. They soon faced heavy rains and strong winds. Lt. Alexander Pearson and his mechanic, Sgt. Royal Atkinson, nearing Cleveland in their DH-4 (#8), experienced "a heavy gust of wind [wind shear] at 4,000 feet which put the plane in a dangerous spin, costing a loss of 2,000 feet before Pearson could regain control."[7] When he finally landed, Pearson avoided serious consequences as his plane skidded dangerously on the slippery runway. His skills would help to make him one of the future winners of the race.

One of the most unusual landings of the entire race occurred next. Lts. Alexander M. Roberts and M.L. Elliott, in their DH-4 (#34) flying from Buffalo to Cleveland, decided to take a shortcut over Lake Erie. When their throttle broke and the Liberty engine sputtered and stopped, they were two miles from shore and three miles east of Ashtabula Harbor. They would have to attempt an inherently dangerous landing on water. Incredibly, the DH-4, not designed as a seaplane, remained buoyant as they landed and they were able to stand on its wings. We don't know how long they could have stayed afloat because a passing freighter had seen them overhead and followed their trajectory. Roberts, an aviator during WWI, had already proven he was a survivor after his wartime experiences of being shot down, captured and confined to a German POW camp. Both men, greatly relieved that they had survived and now without a plane, dropped out of the race.

The forecast of pleasant October weather had indeed been sadly inaccurate, and put those who had left Long Island in the afternoon the preceding day at a distinct disadvantage. After Reynolds and Baz left Buffalo, they encountered strong gale winds and a rainstorm. For safety's sake and at Reynold's insistence, they made an emergency landing in a farmer's field. Three other planes had taken refuge in the same pasture. Baz wrote that if he had been the pilot, he would have continued "and I would have very likely crashed before getting to Cleveland due to the propeller going to pieces in the rain...our untaped propeller was chewed very badly." Propellers, made of wood, functioned best if the tip was covered with doped (glued) fabric, which was missing in the replacement propeller that Reynolds and Bagby had picked up earlier at the control stop in Buffalo. However, even tipped propellers were damaged by heavy rain and suffered further problems, such as the breakdown of the wood, which then threw the plane off balance.

When the wind and rain died down for a spell, Reynolds and Baz flew to Erie, an emergency stop, an hour and 30 minutes away. Near the field at Erie there was a farmhouse where, as Baz later wrote, "We had a good meal and some cider. Also we bought 25 gallons of gas at 40 cents and 4 gallons of oil at $1.25 out of my pocket. It cleared a little in the afternoon and we limped into Cleveland at 1:07 too late to get out to Bryan. We changed propellers at Cleveland and made some minor repairs on the ship."

Other pilots began to drop out. One wrecked his plane by landing on the roof of a farmhouse; another had irreparable engine trouble; and a third, still hoping to remain in the race, was literally stuck in the mud near Elmira, NY.

Maynard was far ahead of them. He had made it as far as Cheyenne, Wyoming, breaking the rules of the race by flying in 25 minutes after sunset, placing him far in front of his rivals in Des Moines, over 500 miles away. In North Platte, Nebraska, on his flight westward, Maynard exchanged greetings with the lead Western pilot, Captain Lowell Smith.

DAY 2: WESTERN AIRMEN

After the Western group left Salt Lake City on October 9, heading east in their open-cockpit planes, they encountered dangerous snow and ice. Lt. Kiel, flying at 12,000 feet, was covered from head to toe with ice and Maj. Spatz, flying a few feet over the railroad line, was nearly blinded from the snow. However, neither pilot was discouraged enough to rest for the 48 hours they were allowed.

Local newspapers reported that pilot Lt. J.C. Richter chose to stay in the race in spite of a wheel having been broken when he missed the field at Rawlins and landed in sagebrush. On the other hand, an injured Lt. S.E. Rice, flying by himself in his SE-5, dropped out of the race after he landed and turned over in a newly planted field near Winnemucca, Nevada, breaking the propeller and damaging one of the wings.

A much worse fate awaited Lieutenants E.V. Wales and William Goldsborough. Caught in a snowstorm near Cheyenne, the pilot, Wales, became disoriented, and seeing the looming wall of a mountain, made a sharp turn. The plane went into a spin and fell into a canyon. Wales fell out and was crushed by his aircraft. An injured Goldsborough tried to stop Wales' bleeding, then wrapped him in clothes, built a fire nearby, and walked three miles through the storm to get help. By the time rescuers returned, Wales had died. He left a grieving fiancée—their wedding, originally planned for October 4, had been postponed until after the race. In reaction to this latest air tragedy, the *Buffalo Express* editorialized, "Is the game worth such sacrifices?" Perhaps America was beginning to lose its taste for the spectacle of an air race with this latest dose of reality.

DAY 3: EASTERN AIRMEN

On the third day of the race, October 10, plane #14, my father's plane, was declared missing from its destination at Chicago. In fact, Reynolds, with Baz clinging to the tail, was attempting to land in a farmer's newly planted field in Michigan while battling wind, rain and fog. In a letter to his mother, Baz described their harrowing experience:

We landed in a muddy wheat field...There is a lot of danger of the ship turning over in mud, so I crawled back on the tail as the Colonel landed it and although the tail came up a little the nose did not go over and we landed successfully. We got chow at a farmhouse and spent the night at Buchanan, Michigan. So many people came out to see the plane that one of us had to stand guard over it while the other slept.

Lt. Belvin Maynard, with his mechanic Sgt. W.E Kline and Trixie at control stop during race. National Archives Photographs 342-FH-3B 7279.

They spent the night with their plane, in the mud of Michigan.

Meanwhile, overnight, the weather had turned cold in Cheyenne, and Maynard faced a frozen overflow pipe, an overheated engine and a damaged radiator that had to be repaired by a local plumber in town. The Red Cross gave both Maynard and Kline a much-needed wool sweater and helmet. Finally ready, and racing against time to make up for a lost five hours, Maynard was delayed again when Trixie hopped out of the cockpit and had to be corralled back into the plane. As the propellers on "Hello Frisco" were turning, the New York Times reported that a spectator yelled, "Parson, the sinners are with you." Maynard kept his lead, arriving in Salduro, Utah, at the end of the day. Well after he completed the race, Maynard wrote in Northeastern North Carolina Stories that he delighted flying over farm and ranch land in the Midwest and western states. He noted that when cattle heard the motor of the plane overhead they would run away, while sheep huddled together, with the "whole mass revolving like the disk of a gramophone."

Maj. A.L. Sneed, two days behind most of the other Eastern flyers, reached Buffalo flying a DH-4.[8] As he approached the field, his observer, Sgt. Worth C. McClure, noticing the muddy field, unbuckled his seat belt and was readying himself to sit on the fuselage near the tail when Sneed landed prematurely with a bump, sending McClure flying. An ambulance arrived but became stuck in the mud, and McClure died before he arrived at the hospital. This was the fifth death in the race.

DAY 3: WESTERN AIRMEN

Capt. Lowell Smith maintained his lead for the Western group heading to New York. Behind him was Lt. Kiel, who arrived in Des Moines, Iowa, 25 minutes before Maj. Spatz. A disorienting rainstorm had delayed Spatz's progress, so that his emergency landing in Hammond, Indiana, to get his bearings, put him behind Kiel. Understandably, the competitive Spatz was not in a good mood when he reached Des Moines and he charged officially that Kiel had left two minutes early from the previous control stop. Kiel was then forced to wait two extra minutes at Des Moines before leaving for Bryan, Ohio. This was not the end of Spatz's irritation. The rivalry continued into New York and would influence both men's decision about continuing in the race.

At the close of Day 3, many of the remaining pilots were unaware that five of their fellow airmen had perished, but the reporters and the Army brass knew what a fatal exercise it had become. The pilots themselves were coming to grips with how dangerous the race was and how much skill, stamina and strength it would take to finish it. For the lucky ones, the triumph outweighed the tragedy.

7

THE FIRST WINNERS

DAY 4: EASTERN AIRMEN

*O*N THE MORNING of October 11, Reynolds and Bagby awoke still stuck in the mud, with sore backs and little sleep. They were anxious to get their plane out of Buchanan, Michigan, and resume the race. They had no idea where their fellow pilots were or that Maynard was close to winning the elapsed time to San Francisco. In his letter home Baz wrote:

> It was raining again in the morning but stopped around 10 AM. In warming up the motor we discovered a leak in the water connections due to a broken hose clamp. A blacksmith made us a new clamp and we filled the radiator, getting away at 11:03 for the 40-minute run into Chicago.
>
> We didn't get out of the wheat field so easily. The plane would not get up speed because of the wheels sinking in the mud and we practically had to stall off with the tail dragging. The colonel is a wonder on landing and taking off on small or muddy fields and is more anxious to be sure of getting into Frisco than of getting a good place in the race.

At Chicago, the makeshift airfield at Grant Park on Lake Michigan was a busy place. Sixteen planes landed and took off, three toward the east, and 13 headed west. The field was covered with reporters. Baz wrote, "We both had broad grins over being safely out of the muddy wheat field and we were asked to hold it for a bunch of snaps and movies." The control stop commander was pleased to report that plane #14 was no longer missing.

In short order, with just the required 30-minute stopovers, plane #14 flew rapidly to Rock Island, Illinois (1:15), to Des Moines, Iowa (1:25), Omaha, Nebraska (1:10), and St. Paul, Nebraska (1:10), where Baz and Reynolds remained the next day for their required Sunday of no flying.

From the hotel in St. Paul, my father explained his working relationship with Reynolds in a letter home:

> I've done very little of the piloting, only to indicate the course when he's fixing his map or goggles. I have much better visibility from the back seat than he has from the front so I usually take the controls so that I can point out the landing fields. Going into Omaha each of us thought the other was driving and the ship flew herself for about a minute. There is no danger in that of course, as neither of us would think of doing any stunts on this trip and the minute she did anything funny we would both have the controls and straighten her up. On all questions of proper course I am boss and he trusts me absolutely and [as] I realize that he's the better pilot we are wasting no time in arguments.

Musing about their bad luck in having an afternoon draw on the first day, Baz wrote:

> If we had gotten out of Mineola [Roosevelt Field] Wednesday morning we would have been ahead of bad weather and a lot further along, even given Maynard a tight squeeze tho his plane is faster than ours. With all our bad luck at Erie and Buchanan there is only one of the afternoon planes out of Mineola that is ahead of us and we intend to catch him tomorrow. When we leave tomorrow morning we will be the 11th plane out of St. Paul for the west, so counting Maynard out there are nine planes between us and Frisco....We are not flying as fast as some but our time is better than most...as we are flying an absolutely

straight course. We passed 3 planes yesterday, all the same speed or faster than we so we...expect to pass 3 more tomorrow.

Ahead of Bagby and Reynolds, another airman, Lt. Earl Manzelman in plane #39, missed the airfield in Salt Lake City and landed in a small field. His first words when he emerged from the cockpit, frozen and confused, were "Where is some hot coffee?"[1]

Belvin Maynard beat out the other Eastern flyers, arriving in a cloudy San Francisco to an awaiting crowd on October 11 at 1:12 p.m. According to Maynard, he would have arrived earlier but he couldn't find the city in the fog and continued flying south. After five minutes he realized his mistake, turned around, headed north and, flying very low, finally saw the tall buildings of San Francisco. He surprised the crowd looking for him in a different direction and then side-slipped to the field. This maneuver may have looked like a flashy demonstration of his skill, but it was, in fact, an effective technique to lose altitude without gaining speed, necessary in the tight quarters of the Presidio Field.[2]

As the first pilot to reach San Francisco, he was heralded as the winner by the press, although the airmen who had left after Maynard on the first day still had a chance to best him for speed. Three top brass of the U.S. Air Service were there to meet him, headed by Maj. Gen. Menoher, Chief of the Air Service. Along with Menoher were two members of the Western Department of the Air Service, Commander General Hunter Liggett and

San Francisco Chronicle, **Oct. 12, 1919. The headline is misleading, since he "won" only the first half of the race for the Eastern pilots from Long Island to San Francisco.**

Aeronautical Officer Col. "Hap" Arnold. Maynard and Kline were escorted to the luxurious Palace Hotel where board and lodging were paid for by the owners. The accommodations were a dramatic change from the straw beds in Chicago and the previous night's spartan accommodations at Salduro, Utah, or any other night of their westbound flight. There is no mention of where Trixie spent the night. Kline explained they had not had a restful night since they began the race: "The roar of the motor is awful, especially when you hear it 12 hours a day...All night long I would be travelling in my sleep."[3] Both Maynard and Kline suffered some deafness from the constant roar of the engine and had trouble hearing the reporters' questions.

Twenty minutes after checking into the hotel and still wearing his dusty, wrinkled uniform, Maynard joined Menoher, Liggett and Arnold at a welcoming luncheon in the elegant dining room of the Palace. The hotel was magnificent. Four years after the 1906 earthquake and fire, the eight-storied, 800-room building had been repaired and refurbished, so that by the 1915 Panama-Pacific International Exposition in San Francisco it was known nationwide for its parties and banquets in the Garden Court, which featured a stained glass domed ceiling and crystal chandeliers from Austria. It had feted President Wilson just weeks before the aviators began arriving and was soon to welcome the King of Belgium.

San Francisco heartily welcomed Maynard and the airmen who followed him. The *San Francisco Chronicle* announced, "City to be Thrown Wide Open to Eastern Airmen Soon to Arrive." Maynard was given a car, invited to luncheons and dinners, and taken on road trips throughout the area. A luncheon and a matinee at the Orpheum were in the plans. And there were requests for him to speak at "every" Baptist church in the city.

DAY 4: WESTERN AIRMEN

Capt. Lowell Smith lost his lead of the Western group on October 11. Given inadequate directions from the previous control stop, he

A confidant 2nd Lt. Kiel arrives at Roosevelt Field before Maj. Spatz. from left: Col. A. Miller, Keil, and Sgt. F.K. McKee. Library of Congress, Bain Collection.

was unable to find the airfield in Cleveland, descended for directions, and landed in a ditch, damaging his landing gear and propeller. Trying to save time, he stuffed his leaking radiator with cornmeal, but still the repairs took five hours and put him way behind Kiel and Spatz who had made it to New York, but not without more squabbles. At Binghamton (the next to last stop), Spatz "asked" the lower ranked Kiel to "delay" his departure for 10 minutes following Spatz's takeoff. Kiel compromised to 5 minutes, but didn't wait to get the authorization of the control stop commander. Ironically Spatz, nearing Long Island, thought he had arrived at Roosevelt Field, but landed at nearby Hazelhurst Field instead. Soldiers ran to his plane to explain his error, and he sped on, landing at the correct field 20 seconds after Kiel. According to the *New York Times*, Lt. Kiel "swooped out of the mists and prepared to land. Immediately a contest in aerial technique began, and Kiel managed to get his plane to the ground twenty seconds before his rival bumped the field in a daring swoop." Both men believed they had won. Kiel's friends weighed in to support their lower-ranked buddy. The decision a day later was left to a group of officers that included Spatz and Kiel. According to the *New York Times,* "Lt. Kiel said he was willing to concede the honor of the first arrival to his friendly rival and the opinion of the officers was that the mistake of Maj. Spatz (landing at the wrong field) would be overlooked." The paper characterized their interchange as an "amicable dispute." Apparently rank had its privileges.

Rome [N.Y.] *Daily Sentinel,* Oct 13, 1919.

Their arrival at 6:30 p.m. at Roosevelt Field put them more than 3 hours behind Maynard's time to San Francisco. A reporter from the *Daily Sentinel* (Rome, NY) described both Spatz and Kiel as "mentally…near exhaustion." When Spatz was asked by a *New York Times* reporter how he felt after his trip, he replied, "How do I feel? To be perfectly frank I feel like a drink of whiskey." He was hesitant about returning to San Francisco. "I don't feel like making the return trip right away. I could, I think, undertake it but I don't want to just now." Kiel was more emphatic. "No one can make me race back to California, and I doubt if I'll ever fly back in the machine. It was a wonderful trip. But the train back will be good enough for me."[4] Kiel complained of the harsh conditions of rain, snow and fog and the inadequacy of his regulation flying clothes (army sweater and leather flying jacket) to protect him from freezing. By the fifth day of the race, the competitive spirit of both Spatz and Kiel had been reduced to near zero.

DAY 5: EAST AND WEST

On Sunday October 12 Maynard rested in San Francisco at the elegant Palace and spoke at two Baptist churches, while Reynolds and Baz caught up with the news of the World Series in their simple hotel in St. Paul, Nebraska. It was a surprise to learn that the odds-on favorite Chicago White Sox had lost to the Cincinnati Reds.

DAY 6: EASTERN AIRMEN

One of the celebrated feats of the race was the successful arrival of Capt. John Owen Donaldson in San Francisco on October 13. His single-seated SE-5 was never built for long distance flying and its 150-horsepower engine was much smaller than the 400 horsepower of the DH-4. In Salduro, Utah, just as Donaldson was about to land, he took off his goggles and oil sprayed into his eye. Temporarily blinded, he lost control and his plane hit the ground hard, damaging his landing gear. Knowing there were no spare parts for his plane, he took a board of pine, created a heavy strut for his landing gear, and headed west.

Lt. Earl Manzelman arrived in San Francisco on the same day in a dramatic manner, thanks to his observer, M.C. Goodnough. In spite of feeling ill with pneumonia, Goodnough crawled out of the cockpit to sit on the tail of the plane. Later it was revealed that he managed this feat so easily because he had "constructed a metal top to the fuselage from the rear cockpit to the tail of his ship. When a landing field is sighted, Goodnough sits up on the edge of the cockpit and lets the wind blow him back against the rudder. He remains in this position and aids in balancing the vessel until it comes to earth."[5] Goodnough had all the makings of a barnstormer; during the race he had also crawled on the wing and dangled from a strut to hold the ship straight. Both Donaldson and Manzelman continued to be frontrunners in the race.

The other pilots not yet in San Francisco did their best to make up time, but troubles continued. Lt. H.D. Norris, flying a DH-4, crashed between St. Paul and North Platte, Nebraska. Another pilot, Lt. J.B. Wright, also in a DH-4, lost his way, following the wrong railroad track, and passed right over Cheyenne at 7:30 p.m., unable to locate the field, although flares, rockets, and a bonfire were used to attract his attention. He landed instead in Stirling, Colorado, with the help of a farmer who signaled him with a flashlight. On landing, he just missed some telegraph poles and wires, impossible to see in the dark. He continued in the race the next day.

Reynolds and Bagby made good time out of St. Paul, flying westward to North Platte, Nebraska (1:10), Sidney, Nebraska (1:10), Cheyenne, Wyoming (:55), Rawlins, Wyoming (1:25), Salt Lake City (3:05) and Salduro, Utah (:50). According to the *Salt Lake Tribune,* Reynolds overshot the field at Salt Lake City and Bagby, seeing a ditch ahead, climbed back on the tail (yet again) to "bring the machine to a halt a few feet from the ditch." They continued on to Salduro and called it a day.

DAY 6: WESTERN AIRMEN

Capt. Lowell Smith completed the one-way trek to Long Island on Monday the 13th, landing at Roosevelt Field in the morning, determined to make the return trip no matter what Spatz and Kiel decided to do. Two others, Lt. H.E. Queen, flying a DH-4, and Lt. R.S. Worthington, in his SE-5, arrived in the afternoon. Worthington had lost his gloves, so his bare hands were raw from exposure.

Another San Francisco airman, D.L. Cardiff, one of two Marine cadets in the race, never made it beyond Salt Lake City. While making an emergency landing near Tampi, Utah, his single-seater Fokker flipped over, breaking the propeller. Marooned in the Utah desert, he was taken in by a Japanese railroad laborer who for four days fed him rice "in every form" for breakfast, lunch, and dinner. He vowed never to eat rice again.[6] Cardiff was finally able to make it to Salt Lake City where, now out of the race, he remained, performing aerial stunts in the area. He had a second unfortunate landing when his plane flipped over again; fortunately, he was not hurt.

DAY 7: EASTERN AIRMEN

Maynard, eager to leave San Francisco for New York, turned down a luncheon invitation from the King of Belgium, but so many people came out to say goodbye at the Presidio Field that he and Kline left later than planned. Maynard's wife, breaking from the traditional stoicism of a U.S. Army wife, had sent him a telegram pleading with him to stop racing. He ignored it. A few days later he would be in serious trouble.

Seven planes arrived in San Francisco from Sacramento on October 14, the same day that Maynard flew out. In plane #14, Baz Bagby piloted the run from Salduro, Utah, to Battle Mountain, Nevada (1:40), to Reno (1:35) and to Sacramento (:55). Reynolds retook the pilot's seat and piloted the plane into San Francisco (:35). Much to their delight, they were not only the ninth plane to finish, but Reynolds' 35 minutes had beaten the previous record set for the Sacramento–San Francisco flight time. (Today, a commercial flight is 20 minutes.)

Maynard, holding Trixie, with Kline. Courtesy of Forsyth County Public Library Photograph Collection, Winston-Salem, NC.

They arrived too late to have a chance to see or speak to Maynard, and settled in the luxurious Palace, along with the other pilots newly arrived in San Francisco. The enforced rest, including a Sunday off, gave the pilots an opportunity to hear each others' stories and talk over whether or not they would continue the race. In the hallways and hotel rooms of the Palace Hotel and in the Pied Piper Bar (being renovated as a tearoom to comply with Prohibition), the airmen exchanged amusing and harrowing stories, and learned of others not so fortunate. Over the "hail fellow well met" atmosphere hung the black shroud of misfortune and tragic deaths.

➤ 8 ◄

TO QUIT OR NOT TO QUIT

OCT. 11–17: EASTERN AIRMEN

BY MID-OCTOBER there were wrecked planes across the entire route of the Transcontinental Air Race. Although many of the remaining Eastern flyers had arrived in San Francisco by then, others were valiantly trying to catch up. Another fatal accident occurred on October 15 at Rigby Ranch in Castle Rock, Utah. Lieutenants French Kirby and Stanley C. Miller, many stops away from San Francisco, were flying west, headed for Salt Lake City, when their plane crashed. The owner of Rigby Ranch, following the progress of the plane above him, told a reporter that he had heard the motor stop while it was at a high altitude and then watched as the plane "floated" downward. "Suddenly at about 200 feet in the air, it banked and dived straight to the ground."[1] Both men perished, prompting even more scathing criticism of the Air Race in the press. The crash was not blamed on the pilots, but on the inadequacy of the engine of the plane—a DH-4. The *Chicago Tribune* editorialized that it was "rank stupidity" to trust the lives of pilots flying planes "with obsolete equipment and structural deficiencies."[2] Fiorello LaGuardia of New York, a former Congressman and WWI pilot, said the race was a "most pathetic display of selfish interests. The toll of death in this race is beyond all expectation." He complained further that the DH-4 was "an obsolete disregarded machine [and] the de Haviland is not a good plane. It was discarded by the English…"[3] Other editorial pages also expressed the obvious: that the race was not portraying flying as a safe form of travel. The American Flying Club urged the U.S. Air Service to halt the race because of the many fatalities.

Why did it proceed? There is no indication that the Air Service

brass even considered stopping it, and the pilots themselves felt two
ways about it.

Wives, fiancées, mothers, and family members of the airmen were
of little consideration to the planners of the race, but relatives, of
course, followed the daily news stories with great anxiety: who was
missing, who had crashed, who was injured, and worst of all, who had
perished. One mother went to see her son after he landed in Salt Lake
City, but missed him by seconds when he took off early. Some family
members waited for hours at the final destinations to welcome their
men home.

Lt. Kiel's fiancé, Miss Elizabeth Case, whose wedding was planned
for Thanksgiving Day, went to the Army Intelligence Office in San
Francisco to wait for news that he had made the one-way trip to Long
Island safely. When Major Spatz's mother and sister greeted him at
Roosevelt Field, his mother insisted on kissing her son, even though
he told her he was too dirty.

The men for their part could assure their families by wire that they
had landed safely at their last control stop of the day, if the control stop
had the facilities to do so. On Sundays, there was time enough to write
home.

One of the pilots broke the clearly understood rule of no flying on
Sunday. Capt. H.C. Drayton, on the heels of Maynard, had problems
with the engine of his DH-4. Heading for Reno, his copilot, 2nd Lt. L.J.
Sweeley, (with whom Drayton shared piloting duties) made an emergency landing on Saturday in Lovelock, Nevada, over 100 miles from
the Reno control stop. On October 14, the *New York Times* reported
that Capt. Drayton, sitting in the copilot seat, anticipated a rough landing in a plowed field and "slid out over the tail...but...suddenly the
ship stood on its nose and sent him hurtling through the air. His heavy
flying outfit prevented serious injury." Drayton decided to fly into Reno
on Sunday and take off with the others at Reno on Monday. Apparently, this was not enough to disbar him from continuing in the race.
Ironically, however, after landing in San Francisco, his copilot refused
to make the round trip. Drayton couldn't find anyone willing to fly

Chicago Tribune, Oct. 16, 1919.

with him and had no choice but to drop out. Although Buz never mentioned Drayton in his letters home, some of the pilots saw the hand of God in this outcome.

A few days later, it was discovered that another pilot, Lt. J.P. Roullett, had broken the rules twice. When he arrived at the Presidio Field on October 16, it was discovered that he had made illegal adjustments to the wiring of his DH-4 so that it would go faster. In doing so he had sacrificed safety for himself and his mechanic, because the plane couldn't fly higher than 9,500 ft. over the mountains. He was ordered to change the wiring so that it would be like all the other DH-4s in the race. (Maynard had also adjusted the wiring of his plane the day before the race; he complied with orders to change the wiring back to its original form, and began the race on time.) Apparently, after a few days rest at the Palace, Roullett left the Presidio field without making all of the required adjustments. He was stopped at the next control stop in Sacramento and ordered back to San Francisco to comply with the rules. By then he didn't have the time to return to the Presidio and remain in the race, so he was, effectively, out. Those pilots who knew that Roullett had altered the wiring of his plane, may have thought something along the lines of "just desserts."

Lt. Maynard almost had cause to regret his decision to make the round trip. Two days after he left San Francisco, ahead of all the other

Eastern airmen, the engine of his DH-4 stopped en route to Omaha. Making an emergency landing on October 16, he and Kline discovered the cause: a broken crankshaft. Any other man would have called it a day, but not Maynard, who was aware that Capt. Roy Francis on his way to San Francisco had wrecked his Martin Bomber in Nebraska. Francis's plane had an engine like his own. Maynard ran to a farmhouse, called the Omaha airfield, and found out that Capt. Francis's plane was only 11 miles away. He convinced Francis to help him, borrowed a truck and arranged to have the engine of the Martin Bomber trucked to his plane. The DH-4 was pushed underneath a tree and hoisted up while "locals" directed car headlights on to the scene as Maynard's master mechanic, Sgt. Kline, switched engines during the night. An exhausted Kline slept in the seat behind Maynard on the next leg, Trixie presumably on his lap.

Word travelled fast. Second Lt. Pearson, who had demonstrated his skills with a safe landing on a slippery field in Cleveland, hoped that Maynard's poor luck would be his chance to take the lead on the return trip, but he, too, had bad luck, with a broken motor in North Platte which delayed him three days. As it was, Maynard lost more hours than Pearson, putting Pearson in the lead in actual flying time. Maynard meanwhile arrived in Chicago on October 17. At Grant Park, the crowd of 3,000 was made up of newspaper photographers, cameramen, members of the Red Cross, and committees of welcome. The *Chicago Tribune* reporter described his takeoff as "the most sensational seen in Grant Park. With the wind on his tail and fifty feet off the ground nosed her straight up...every pilot on the field caught his breath, and wondered if—but the ship did not stall." He then took the more dangerous route east across Lake Michigan to save time.

OCT. 15–17: WESTERN AIRMEN

Meanwhile, the San Francisco pilots who had reached New York were rethinking their decision about whether to make the round trip. In spite of both Spatz's and Keil's protestations about continuing the race, first Spatz and then Kiel changed their minds. Without sharing his plans with his fellow aviators from San Francisco, Spatz went out to Roosevelt Field on September 15, inspected his plane, and then readied himself to depart. Meanwhile Capt. Lowell Smith, seeing Spatz warming up, dashed to his own plane. Spatz left at 2:28 pm and Smith was right behind him at 2:31 pm. The two competitors were neck and neck, but Smith made it to Buffalo three stops away and Spatz did not. As Smith's plane was being checked out by mechanics that evening, it caught fire from a lantern and was destroyed. Now without a plane, Smith waited for Spatz to arrive, hoping he could convince the major to quit the race and give his plane to him. Two days later, October 17, Spatz finally arrived in Buffalo, and, surprisingly, in response to Smith's pleading, gave up his plane. Spatz was now out of a plane and out of the race. "I suggested the trade," Smith told a reporter from the *San Francisco Chronicle.* At first Spatz refused to listen to the idea, and then he came around. "He was dog-tired while I had had some rest." Earlier Smith had told another reporter, "I talked him out of it....I wanted to fly bad and he was simply good enough to give me his ship and his chance." Smith sped on to Chicago arriving the same day.

Maj. J.C.P. Bartholf arrives at Roosevelt Field in SE-5.

While a few pilots were making the round trip, others were just completing the one-way race. The day Smith's plane was destroyed by fire, Western airman Maj. J.C. Bartholf approached New York. In sole control of his SE-5, Bartholf's trouble began just out of Rochester en route to Binghamton. Writing his own account of what happened, he noted that the weather forced him down to "skimming along scarcely over the hilltops."[4] After waiting for the weather to clear, he left for Long Island, only to turn back because of the rain. The next day began more auspiciously, but as he finally approached Long Island, he saw two different airfields adjacent to each other and didn't know which was the right one. His anxious wife and mother, who were on the field to welcome him, could see his difficulty as he circled over Hazelhurst and Roosevelt Fields for eight minutes. They took out their handkerchiefs and began waving to catch his attention. Soon officers on the field, including control commander Col. Archie Miller, and newspaper reporters, were all waving handkerchiefs and newspapers. At long last they caught his eye and he landed safely in the right place.

One of Bartholf's first questions to Col. Miller was whether the other pilots from San Francisco were returning. His next question was how many days and hours did he have before it was necessary for him to leave for San Francisco and still be within the rules of the race. Told he had 96 hours plus Sunday meant that as long as he left Roosevelt Field by Monday, October 20, he would still be a contestant. Next, he needed permission to leave New York so that he could attend the undefeated Harvard football team's game on October 18 in Boston. Permission was granted, he attended the game, and his alma mater won, beating Brown University 7–0. (Harvard went on to win the Rose Bowl in January.) The Class of 1913 alumni notes report that Bartholf visited Cambridge before leaving for San Francisco by plane. However, for reasons unknown, he did not continue in the race.

While Bartholf was finalizing his plans to attend the Harvard football game, pilots H.E. Queen, R.S. Worthington and Emil Kiel were still considering their options. Then, on October 17, two days after Spatz and Smith had left for San Francisco, Lt. Kiel was back again in the race. He climbed into the cockpit of the same plane, now with a rebuilt engine, in which he had left San Francisco nine days earlier. Lts. Queen and Worthington also left the same day for their return trip back to San Francisco. Only one of the three would eventually make it to the Presidio Field. Worthington had a scare when he landed at Buffalo and discovered that someone at Binghamton, the previous control stop, had tampered with his plane using a nail to make three holes in his fuel tank. It could have had dangerous consequences. Fortunately it was a short leg, a mere 20 minutes between Binghamton and Buffalo, and he landed safely. It was the only act of vandalism reported during the race.

OCT. 18–20: EASTERN AIRMEN

Belvin Maynard reached Roosevelt Field early on the afternoon of October 18, making him the first pilot to complete the round trip. Maynard's landing at Buffalo hours earlier had been executed with typical flourish. Instead of circling the field (required by the race committee) the *Salt Lake Tribune* described a "series of banks and side slips which brought him down quickly to a neat landing." Later, true showman that he was, he repeated his landing technique at Roosevelt Field in front of a crowd of well-wishers, including his wife and daughters. After deplaning he made a point of praising his mechanic, Sgt. Kline. Trixie ran around the plane barking, then jumped into an automobile, no doubt grateful that her long ordeal in her master's plane was over.

Newspapers declared Maynard the winner of the race for both elapsed time and actual flying time from east to west, and for elapsed time for the round trip. This can only have been dispiriting to all those remaining Eastern flyers, particularly those who hadn't left San Francisco yet for the trip back to Long Island.

Also dispiriting to Baz and the others at the Palace Hotel were the tales of newly arrived airmen. Lt. G.B. Newman and Capt. A.H. Page of the Marine Corps had been stuck in mud for five days. While making an emergency landing near Salduro, Utah, on October 13, their DH-

4 had flipped over on its back, breaking the propeller, bending the radiator, damaging the wings, and demolishing the rudder—all held fast in deep mud. Farmers brought tractors only to have their machines also become stuck in the mud. Fortunately, a nearby locomotive was able to pull the plane two miles to dry ground. The pilots obtained a new propeller and made the necessary repairs themselves. They flew back to Salt Lake City to test the trustworthiness of their repairs, and then continued the race, arriving in San Francisco late in the afternoon of October 18, ready to tell their story to fellow airmen.

Equally as harrowing was the experience of Capt. Felix Steinle, who had crash-landed in Cheyenne, Wyoming. A fire broke out and he became wedged in his seat. He escaped only through the strength of his sergeant, H. Myhres, who pulled him to safety. Apparently Steinle had broken three ribs, but all he knew was that he hurt. They were given another plane and continued west to Rawlins and Green River. As they approached the field at Green River, the wheels touched the ground, but Steinle was afraid he couldn't land safely, so he gunned the motor and continued on toward Salt Lake City. Concerned about not having enough gasoline, he landed at Kamas, Utah, where he picked up fuel, and then went on to Salt Lake City on October 17, where he limped off the plane. A day later he was at the Palace Hotel recreating his experiences for fellow aviators.

Lt. D.B. Gish, one of most courageous of pilots, also arrived in San Francisco on the 18th. He had proven his valor from the first day of the race when he landed his plane after it went up in flames east of Buffalo, and then continued in another plane. On his way to California, Gish made five forced landings, two of them "dead stick landings" because the Liberty engine in his DH-4 had died. At Salt Lake City he lost a wheel at takeoff, yet landed successfully at Salduro, the next control stop. When he reached San Francisco, he came in with too much speed. His plane struck a frame building and was wrecked. The reporter for the *San Francisco Chronicle* commented that, "Gish, who has emerged alive from more airplane crashes than almost any other man in the flying game, made a deal with the control commander" (Col. "Hap"

Arnold) to take over the DH-4 of Lt. George, who had decided not to return, even though he was second behind Maynard. Gish then continued in the race in his third plane.

Some of the less harrowing and more endearing escapades involved planes that were lost and flying off course over Iowa, Nebraska, Utah and Wyoming, surprising and delighting farmers, ranchers, teachers and schoolchildren. One such aviator, hopelessly lost on October 18, flew over ranches in Daggett County, Utah, in the Uinta Mountains on the border with Wyoming. One observer noted the "whirring motor brought out of doors most of the people of the county. Fifty miles from the nearest railroad and far distant from any center where aeroplanes had been seen, winged one of the great machines, with its motor punctuating its otherwise noiseless passage above the mountains. [It was] startling to hear the sputters of the engine high above the town where [typically] the only noises were those of a threshing machine or an occasional automobile."[5] The residents of Burnt Fork, hearing the plane overhead, called authorities in the next town, Manila, where school was dismissed so that the children could have their first look at an airplane.

Another pilot, Lt. L.V. Beau Jr., heading for Salt Lake City on October 20, was off course south of Evanston, Wyoming. He landed in a hayfield next to a schoolhouse, delighting the children, who tried to climb on board. His plane remained in the hayfield, much to the joy of the townsfolk, while his mechanic, Private J.J. McVeigh, rode a borrowed horse to the closest telegraph station to contact the field in Salt Lake City.

October 19 was a Sunday, another forced rest day. In light of all that had happened to both the Eastern and Western airmen, we can appreciate that there were continual discussions about whether to complete the round trip. The longer the Eastern flyers stayed at the Palace Hotel, with its many amenities, the harder it may have been for them to decide to continue. Furthermore, the availability and comfort of the train from San Francisco to New York was enticing to exhausted men. Baz's letter home to his mother explained that even with Sunday off, the pilots were allowed 96 hours of non-flying time in San Francisco, where he had had "a wonderful rest."

The pilots in San Francisco who chose not to make the round trip were given train tickets home. The fastest train to New York made it in 85 hours and 55 minutes, a trip free of worry, with a dining car and a cup of coffee whenever they wanted, and sleeping berths if they were travelling first class. For the 14 who opted for the train, it is not known which weighed most heavily in their decision: exhaustion, lack of sleep, the constant noise during flight, inadequate landing fields, poor maps, little advance information on conditions at the next control stop, weather, bad luck in starting time at Long Island, pleas from their family, a lost sense of adventure after fellow airmen perished, or a loss of competitive spirit after Maynard reached Long Island. Baz chose to continue in the race. His cohort John Reynolds chose the train.

OCT. 20–31: EASTERN AIRMEN

Twelve of the 26 Eastern flyers, including Baz, Steinle, Gish and Hartney, chose to make the round trip. Four of them had already left: Maynard, Capt. John Owen Donaldson, flying his SE-5, with its self-repaired landing gear, Lt. Pearson, and Lt. Manzelman with his observer Goodnough. Just six of these 12 would successfully complete the race within the time limit.

Why did they choose to continue? My father's choice seemed simple: he hadn't had a chance to prove that he could pilot a plane across the country, since he had only piloted three segments on the trip west. He and others may have felt an obligation to finish what they said they were going to do. Many thrived on competition, and had confidence they would be successful. We don't know if they were expecting any kind of reward, such as money, gifts or a trophy. Those who had competed in the Toronto race were not allowed to receive cash, although they could accept gifts. Neither pilots' memoirs nor my father's letters ever mentioned a reward.

Gish's troubles as well as his resourcefulness continued. He de-

Control stop at Cheyenne with Lt. Gish's #10 plane with hand-painted "JUNK" on side.

scribed his misadventures in his report after the race to the Director of the Air Services. On the return trip to Long Island and still over San Francisco Bay his motor began misfiring, and throughout his return the radiator presented continuous problems. At Rawlins, Wyoming, a 35-mile-an-hour crosswind necessitated three attempts before Gish was able to set his DH-4 down, and then it was on rough terrain: a wheel gave way and he broke the propeller, radiator, part of the back support, and the leading edge of the upper and lower left wings. The plane was repaired and equipped with a new radiator, wheel and propeller. Due to landing on rough ground, much of the plane had to be replaced, including parts of the upper and lower wings. Ingeniously "by cutting out sections of two wings from planes of other crashes we built our own wings."[6] All this took two days and by then there was a foot of snow on the ground. Undaunted, Gish sped off and landed in Cheyenne covered in ice. There he had to solder the radiator and change the propeller once again. His plane was photographed at Cheyenne with the word "JUNK" prominently painted on the fuselage. No wonder. As he continued on his return, flying eastward from Cheyenne to Des Moines, he had to re-solder the radiator three times. Trying to make Chicago and finish the race by October 31, Gish had to make a forced landing at Naperville, Illinois, due to a broken air pump assembly and damaged radiator. The location was 27 miles outside of Chicago. His DH-4 was living up to its JUNK label. Unfortunately, there is no photo of the three horses that pulled his plane out of the field. Before he left for Chicago he had also repaired the motor, but problems continued, necessitating "three forced landings at Chicago owing to motor trouble." Apparently, nothing was going to stop him.

Back in San Francisco, Baz, now lead pilot in plane #14, selected a mechanic, Sgt. Lee N. Parrish, to join him on the return trip to New York. Parrish had flown out with Lt. Harold H. George in plane #16, coming in second after Maynard in the race from New York to San Francisco. Lt. George elected to return by train ceding his plane to Gish.

Baz wrote to his mother that he would take the return slowly, as he was "only interested in getting the plane safely back to Langley," his home field. Now that he was in charge, the brash young copilot, who during the trip out would have elected to fly to Cleveland with a damaged propeller, was now less interested in proving what he could do, and more inclined to look after his ship, and his health and safety, as well as that of Sgt. Parrish.

After leaving San Francisco on October 20, Parrish wanted to drop a letter off to his family in Galt, California, southeast of Sacramento. It is likely that they followed the Lincoln Highway between San Francisco and Sacramento, which would have taken them east over Oakland, Hayward, Dublin, Livermore, and Tracy on what is now Highway 580; then north to Stockton, Galt and finally Mather Field outside of Sacramento. After literally dropping off the first airmail letter the Parrish family had ever received, they flew in and out of Sacramento and began climbing. Baz did not find the trip over the Sierra difficult. He had agreed to take a dog to Reno, and the poor dog sat shivering uncontrollably in Parrish's lap at 14,000 feet.

After Reno, Baz avoided the direct route over more mountain ranges and flew to Battle Mountain by staying down in the winding valley of the Humboldt River. Heading for Salduro he then climbed again to 11,000 feet over the "straight jagged edges of rock, too steep for the snow to stick on." When he landed after sunset on the hard salt field at Salduro he bent an axle and blew a tire. Farther east, Capt. J.O. Donaldson in his SE-5 was the second after Maynard to complete the return flight arriving October 22 at Roosevelt Field, Long Island. This was quite a feat since a reporter from the *Salt Lake Tribune* had written on October 17 that Donaldson had admitted his plane was not safe at high altitudes and offered to wager that he wouldn't make it safely to Long Island.

Baz continued to Salt Lake City, then headed to Wyoming. Flying to Rawlins he battled snow and a 50-mile-per-hour wind. At the control stop he learned that a storm was coming in; he decided to skip Cheyenne because of its high elevation of 6400 ft. and fly straight for Sidney, Nebraska, at 4000 ft. He knew he would he be penalized by the race committee for missing a control stop, but chose safety instead. They landed at sundown, and spent two nights in Sidney waiting for the weather to change. His five-page letter to his father was written on the stationery of the Sidney Hotel which stated its amenities in caps: "HOT AND COLD WATER. TELEPHONE SERVICE. STEAM HEAT. ELECTRIC LIGHTS" and some advice to hotel guests: "MAKE THIS YOUR SUNDAY TOWN." There, Baz wrote "We got in here last night but it's been very foggy and rainy all day...I'm not racing and I don't want to go too far during the day as it's not worth the strain. It's not that I'm being lazy Dad, but after too much flying it's hard to sleep well. I'm in good condition and could easily stand twice as much flying as we've done any day yet."

Baz hoped to do the return trip in tandem with Lt. Col. Hartney, who was at North Platte, Nebraska, one stop ahead of him, flying solo in his German Fokker. Baz wrote, "I'm sure I can catch up with him as my ship is faster."

On October 23, an alarming AP report was published in the *Laramie Republican*. "Bagby and Gish airplanes were wrecked this morning.

Control stop at Rock Island, Illinois. Sign says "Welcome to Rock Island." National Archives 342-FH-3B7278.

The Gish machine can be repaired, but the Bagby machine is so badly damaged that it will have to be shipped. Fliers uninjured." The headline in the *Ogden Standard* trumpeted the reason: "Planes Wrecked Near Rawlins in Strong Wind. ...The gale caught the Bagby plane as it was lifting from the ground, carried the machine into a fence, smashing propeller, wings and gear." Later his family learned to their relief that the report was *not* about Baz's plane. If the news was accurate about Gish, it offers another example of his not letting anything get in his way, since he continued in the race.

On that same day two other Eastern pilots, Alexander Pearson and Earl H. Manzelman, arrived at Roosevelt Field having avoided much of the treacherous weather that held up Baz and Hartney. It was an exciting finish for them: they left Cleveland at the same time, at Buffalo Pearson was ahead by three minutes, and by the time Pearson arrived in Long Island he was 17 minutes ahead of Manzelman. According to the *New York Times*, Manzelman arrived at the field with his observer, M.C. Goodnough, who repeated his daring feat of "clinging to the tail to give the plane better balance as it landed..."

Although the bad weather persisted in Nebraska, Baz and Parrish flew to North Platte on October 24, and spent three nights there, including a Sunday when they had to stop flying anyway. There they met Hartney. They left for St. Paul, Nebraska, on October 27, in fog and sleet. Baz's air speed indicator froze and there was ice on the wings, but he had better luck than Hartney, who, on his way to St. Paul, made a forced landing at Poole, Nebraska, where it was determined that he had a life-threatening100 pounds of ice on his plane, including his propeller, which was coated with it.

The weather improved the following day, and Baz and Parrish made up time as they flew from St. Paul to Omaha, on to Des Moines, and Rock Island, Illinois, arriving in Chicago in formation with Hartney, landing five minutes before him.

On October 29, encouraged by better weather and their camaraderie, Baz, Parrish and Hartney were determined to finish the race in the allotted time limit. They left Chicago at 6:34 a.m. and 6:40 a.m. respectively and raced from Chicago to Bryan, Ohio, Cleveland, Buffalo, and Rochester, arriving after sundown in Binghamton. On these flights Baz and Parrish were ahead of Hartney by only a few minutes until their arrival in Binghamton; there they purposely flew in with a showy nose-to-nose.

I left Chicago early yesterday morning at the same time as Colonel Hartney left in his Fokker and I've held back just a little so that we could come in together. He has the most reliable bus, but mine is faster. We will land in N.Y. side by side with the colonel a few seconds ahead. We practiced a little combat over the field here before landing and he put it all over me. We would have made New York easily but were held up overtime at all control stops due to their being unable to give us gas and oil on time. In cold weather the oil is as stiff as molasses and they wouldn't bother to warm it up.

The *Binghamton Morning Sun* of October 30 headlined their ar-

On his return Baz is met by his older brother, U.S. Navy Lt. Commander Oliver Bagby.

rival, marveling, "It has been the closest race of two machines in the great aviation event...with Col. Hartney in the lead, and Bagby 30 seconds behind him."

Stymied by bad weather the next day, they couldn't leave until October 31, the last day of the race. It was my father's choice to let Hartney come in first. Arriving at Roosevelt Field, the *Binghamton Press* reported on the "lively air battle 20 seconds apart." They landed with only five hours to spare before the deadline. Baz's San Francisco to Long Island time was 24 hours, 27 minutes and 21 seconds, which he wrote was "among the best," averaging 115 mph. Baz and Hartney joined the other four Eastern flyers (Maynard, Donaldson, Pearson and Manzelman) who had completed the trip in the allotted time. Baz telegraphed his family that he had made it safely. In his letter to his mother the next day he wrote, "I am very tired of travelling around and will be glad to get back to the home field."

OCT. 20–31: WESTERN AIRMEN

Both Lt. Kiel and Lt. Queen dropped out of the race on October 20. Kiel wrecked his plane 12 miles out of Sidney, Nebraska, 1,088 miles from his goal. Both Lt. Queen and Capt. Smith had left Rawlins, Wyoming, at the same time, but Queen's plane was felled with a burned-out engine in Tipton, Wyoming, with only 809 miles left of his journey. Now there were just two airmen in the race from San Francisco, Capt. Lowell Smith and Lt. R.S. Worthington.

On October 21, a victorious Capt. Smith was the first of the Western airmen to complete the round trip from San Francisco. He told the press that according to his logbook he had beaten Maynard in the actual flying time coast to coast. San Francisco went all out to welcome Smith home. He and his mechanic, Emmett Tanner (formerly Spatz's mechanic) had their picture in the *San Francisco Chronicle*, along with an article with a few details of their trip. Smith claimed he had been "plagued by bad luck." Now he was "dead tired, but happy." He had a chance to sleep a few hours at the Palace before a formal reception at City Hall. Col. "Hap" Arnold spoke, a letter from Smith's father was read, and the mayor extolled Smith to the audience: "I present an American hero. I present you a Californian, a young man born in Santa Barbara, one whose name will be placed on the pages of history to be written for the fact that he piloted an American

Col. "Hap" Arnold signs in Capt. Smith at the Presidio. Courtesy of Golden Gate National Recreation Area, Park Archives (Crissy Field History Study Collection GOGA 35263).

airplane [actually it was British designed] safely through dizzy heights, rain and snowstorm to New York City and back again." Smith dreaded public speaking, but he garnered enough courage to thank the

Capt. Lowell Smith (left) lands at Presidio with his mechanic Sgt. Emmett Tanner. *San Francisco Chronicle*, October 22, 1919.

crowd, commenting on how well he was received along the route and his pleasure at being home again. He had a large cut on his forehead from a piece of ice, which most likely flew off the propeller during his flight home. After the reception, a movie was made of his receiving a gold medal from the city. Ten days later, the last day of the race,

Capt. Lowell Smith lands his DH-4 (Bluebird) at the Presidio. Courtesy of Golden Gate National Recreation Area, Park Archives (Crissy Field History Study Collection GOGA 35263).

Lt. Worthington arrived in San Francisco in his SE-5 with little fanfare. The race was over but the headlines continued.

POST OCT. 31

Lt. Belvin Maynard, "the flying parson," made news again over an unfortunate remark about alcohol being the source of the problem for many wrecks and some deaths in the Air Race. In short order, this damning comment was broadcast by the Anti-Saloon League, and immediately denied by the Air Service brass, who claimed that, "At every control stop the flyers and mechanics were examined by officers, in the same manner as the engines." Maynard said his comments had been "juggled," which was denied by an official of the Anti-Saloon League. There was talk of court-martialing Maynard. From December 1–22, the *New York Times* kept this controversy alive, along with Maynard's criticisms of New York women for their scanty clothes and frivolity. The last entry in the *Times* reported that Maynard would leave the Army and follow his earlier calling to the ministry and return to the pulpit. It was an unexpected ending to his breathtaking success in the Air Race.

Just weeks after the race, Baz had his first crash flying his DH-4 in the fog near Langley Field. Attempting to land in the dark, he hit a tree, crashed into a ditch, and broke the landing gear and propeller. Miraculously, he was not hurt. The following day he took Sgt. Parrish back to the area to see the wreck, and together they salvaged the propeller that had gotten them through the return trip from San Francisco to New York. This is the propeller that is still in my family's basement, almost 100 years later. If the First Transcontinental Reliability and Endurance Test were to have a logo, it would have to be a broken propeller.

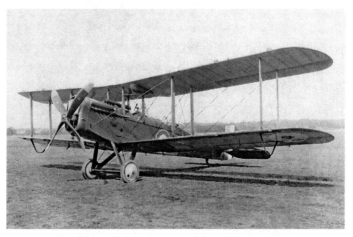

9

R E S U L T S   A N D
R E P E R C U S S I O N S

IRST THERE WAS the naming of the winners and their awards. Then the inevitable questions: Had General Billy Mitchell achieved his goals? Was the Transcontinental Air Race worth the loss of lives? The press, Air Race organizers, military brass, and Congress all weighed in on these issues. The very future of the U.S. Army Air Service was at stake.

Out of the 59 entries, only eight pilots finished the round trip race in time: six from the East (1st Lt. Baz Bagby, Capt. J.O. Donaldson, Lt. Col. H.E. Hartney, 2nd Lt. E.H. Manzelman, 1st Lt. B. Maynard, and Lt. Alexander Pearson) and two from the West (Capt. Lowell Smith and 2nd Lt. R.S. Worthington). Lt. Belvin Maynard, flying a DH-4, won in most of the official race categories but not all of them. The winner of the round trip actual flying time was Eastern pilot 2nd Lt. Alexander Pearson in plane #8, also a DH-4. In spite of taking off from Roosevelt Field three hours after Maynard on the first day of the race, Pearson's round-trip flying time of 48 hours, 14 minutes and 18 seconds beat Maynard's by 20 hours. When Pearson was asked by a reporter if he had had any remarkable experiences during the trip, he laughed and said, "Yes, I got there and back." Second place went to Capt. Lowell Smith, flying a DH-4 Bluebird from San Francisco, who finished the

FACING PAGE, TOP TO BOTTOM: SE-5, a single-seater British plane flown during the Transcontinental Air Race by three pilots, and by Baz in 1921. Wing span 27 ft., length 20ft. 11in., maximum speed 122 mph. (Wikipedia) • DH-4, an American plane, the one most frequently flown in the Air Race. Wing span 34 ft., length 31 ft., maximum speed 128 mph. (USAF) • Fokker D VII, a single-seater German plane flown by Col. Hartney in the Air Race. Wing span 29 ft., length 22.81 ft., maximum speed 115 mph depending on the model. (National Museum of USAF) trip in 54 hours, 14 minutes and 13 seconds. Maynard was sixth, completing the course in 68 hours, 29 minutes and 58 seconds. However, because Maynard was the first of the Long Island group to reach San Francisco and the first to return to Long Island, he was greeted on both coasts with much fanfare and press as if he had won the race.

Maynard did win the actual one-way flying time from Long Island to San Francisco (25 hours, 16 minutes, 47 seconds) for the Eastern group, followed by Lt. H.H. George and 2nd Lt. Alexander Pearson. The one-way elapsed time (3 days, 6 hours, 47 minutes, 11 seconds) was also won by Maynard, with Pearson next, followed by Capt. John O. Donaldson (the only one in this elite first group to fly an SE-5).

As for the Western, San Francisco to Long Island, group, the actual one-way flying time to New York (25 hours, 23 minutes, 19 seconds) was won by Lt. Worthington, flying an SE 5, followed by 2nd Lt. Emil Kiel in a DH-4 and Maj. Carl Spatz in a DH-4 Bluebird. Spatz won the elapsed time for the trip to the East Coast (3 days, 8 hours, 40 minutes, 35 seconds.) Kiel was a close second (3 days, 8 hours, 43 minutes, 20 seconds) and Smith was third.

The winner of the Endurance Test (all pilots who completed the round-trip within the time limit without changing motors) was Capt. John Donaldson flying an SE-5, followed by 2nd Lt. E.H. Manzelman in a DH-4. Lt Col. Reynolds and Lt. Bagby in the DH-4 were listed 4th, behind Col. Hartney in the captured German Fokker.

The Air Service computed the status of each pilot on the basis of a point system not revealed before the race. Points were given to only the top three in each category. The first-place winner in each category received three points, the second two points and the third one point. Maynard acquired the most points, so that the Air Service decreed he was the winner. Pilots grumbled about the Air Service decision of who won the one way elapsed time, believing that Maynard had had an unfair advantage by being one of the earliest to take off, and not having to wait for gasoline at the control stops. However, since this was a U.S. Army test, decided by generals, lower ranked men made no written complaints, and they accepted the results.

The six Eastern pilots and the two Western pilots who completed the race were elated to know that their names would be engraved on the prestigious Mackay Trophy as the Best Airmen of 1919. The previous year, the Mackay Trophy had been awarded to just one pilot, Capt. Edward V. Rickenbacker, for downing 26 German planes in WWI. The Trophy, established in 1911 by Clarence H. Mackay, head of the Postal Telegraph-Commercial Cable Companies, honors pilots for "meritorious flight, gallantry, intrepidity, initiative, resourcefulness, and unusual presence of mind under combat or non-combat conditions."

For 1919, Lt. Maynard and Lt. Pearson head the list. Two pilots, Lt. Gish and Capt. Steinle, whose many mishaps proved they were up to every challenge during the race, did not finish in the allotted time, but were awarded the Mackay Trophy anyway. This was a surprising and unexpected disregard for military rules; it probably occurred because the race was co-sponsored by the non-military American Flying Club of New York, an organization less concerned with military protocol.

Gish had made it to Chicago on October 31, the last day of the race. He continued his flight to Cleveland arriving after dark, five control stops from his goal and his dream of being one of the winners. The next day, November 1, instead of flying to Long Island, Gish flew directly to Washington D.C. Why? His month's leave from Walter Reed Hospital was almost up. Did he return to the hospital? Did he contact the sisters who had kissed him just before his departure on the first day of the race? Did he return to motorcycle racing? At some point, Gish put on a two-week demonstration of stunt flying for the patients at Walter Reed. Other than that his trail is cold at the end of the race, as is Steinle's, who made it as far as Chicago before the deadline. It is satisfying to know that the courage of both Gish and Steinle was appreciated and acknowledged by the American Flying Club.

Winners could not keep the Trophy. It remains on display at the Smithsonian Air and Space Museum in Washington D.C., with the winning names added each year. Ten years after the race, Clarence Mackay decided that the pilots in the race should have something tangible to show that they were award winners. So, in 1929, my father and the others received a gold medal with an engraving of the Trophy on one side and their name and rank on the other.

What about cash prizes? In the earlier air race between Long Island and Toronto in August 1919, none of the pilots in the U.S. Army Air Service were allowed to receive money; one donor gave them gold watches instead. The *Chicago Tribune* on October 21 reported that for those who raced in the Transcontinental Race there would be no cash prizes for the winners. Nevertheless, many donors contributed cash: four $1000 prizes were given by the Packard Automobile Company, Manufacturers Aircraft Association, Edward Desus, and the Fisher Body Company, and two $500 prizes were donated by the Ford Automobile Company and Charles A. Comiskey, owner of the White Sox. Lesser amounts or gifts from others included a Parker Shot Gun (valued at $200) from Abercrombie & Fitch, a leather flying suit (valued at $100) from Brooks Brothers, and a gold cigarette case ($150) and silver wristwatch ($50) from Brewster and Goldsmith Company. The Air Service and the American Flying Club divvied up the gifts and cash, with Maynard and Pearson receiving the most. Maynard was given the gun, Pearson the leather flying suit, Donaldson the gold cigarette case, and Gish the silver wristwatch. All the winners received Liberty Bonds ranging from $256 to $1,025 (from $3,746 to $14,995 in 2017 currency). The mechanics, so essential to the success of the pilots, particularly Maynard's ace mechanic, Sgt. Kline, did not receive any recognition, except from the grateful pilots themselves.

Survivors of the race explained their good fortune differently. Maynard credited his success to the use of his compass (enabling him to fly above the clouds). Not revealed during the race, but included in articles Maynard later wrote for the Raleigh, North Carolina *News and Observer*, he explained that by using his compass he was able to shorten his flight by flying over both Lake Erie ("100 miles over open water") and Lake Michigan, as well as over the mountains outside of Cheyenne. At Cheyenne, the control stop commander warned him many times not to fly over the mountains. Maynard may have listened to this advice until he realized he could save 75 miles by ignoring it. "When you are racing, every mile counts so I soon changed my mind and headed west across the mountains." Maynard also praised the skills of his mechanic, Sgt. Kline, as crucial to his success. But Maynard was also canny and not afraid to bend the rules, as he did when he landed at the Cheyenne control stop after sunset. He put himself way ahead of his competitors on the first day and remained there even after two serious mishaps that took hours to repair.

Luck also played a role in Maynard's success: his early morning departure the first day meant he did not have to compete with other pilots for fuel, supplies or attention at the control stops, and by luck, he flew predominately in clear weather, while later flyers encountered storm conditions. Maynard knew his engine vibrated between 1,400–1,500 rpm, so he cruised at 1,550, gaining considerable speed on minimal engine strain. Maynard was considered an excellent mechanic himself and had grown up repairing farm machinery on his family's farm. This, too, was a factor in his success.

Capt. John Donaldson, flying solo in his SE-5, had his own strategy. At a dinner given in his honor at the American Flying Club he said he flew by "instinct" and did not have to use a compass because he flew so low. He travelled "as near the ground as possible" and "sought the protection of every little hill...In crossing the Rockies instead of flying above the peaks I frequently skimmed through the passes at an elevation of only 25' above the rocks."[1] Lt. Alexander Pearson profited from Donaldson's strategy by cleverly using him as his compass as he flew high above him![2]

Although not one of the winners, Maj. John Bartholf, also flying solo in an SE-5, had a winning strategy for surviving, and not being one of the many wrecks. He wrote, "This is a reliability race. Which means, rely on yourself."[3] His careful preparation before the race included superintending the installation of the motor, checking every part on his plane a week before taking off, and stocking his plane with a supply of tools and spare parts. During the race, he inspected each airfield after arriving to prepare for his takeoff the next day. At the control stop in

Rawlins he chose to sleep in a shack with the nose of his plane in the door so that it wouldn't freeze!

Solving the problem of inadequate maps, Lt. Lewis S. Webster, an Eastern pilot flying a DH-4, mounted his maps on cardboard 10 inches by 18 inches and added the compass course, distance and other details. He explained, "The difficulty of finding the designated landing fields could have been avoided if each pilot had been furnished a blueprint showing the exact location of the field with references to nearby points."[4]

John Reynolds profited from his days as the aerial observer for the Transcontinental Truck Convoy of 1919, which travelled on existing roads over most of the same terrain as the Air Race. He was level-headed, took minimal risks, and was fortunate in his choice of copilot, my father, Baz Bagby, who may have saved Reynolds' life twice by climbing on the fuselage to hold down the tail of the plane at landing. Bagby (like Maynard) knew his way around machines, having repaired machinery at his father's tree nursery. On his return trip from San Francisco to New York, Bagby averaged 115 mph, and at 24 hours, 27 minutes, 21 seconds, his time was second in speed, beating all pilots except Pearson. He felt he was aided by his choice of a non-vibrating speed of 1630 rpm. Lt. Gish and Capt. Steinle credited their success to never giving up despite numerous setbacks. Col. Hartney's flying skills, honed during WWI, and his knowledge of his plane's idiosyncrasies, got him out of a number of dangerous situations.

Although none of the successful airmen had had previous exposure to ice on their planes and themselves, they persevered, got themselves a cup of hot coffee at their next stop and "soldiered" on. In general, the survivors had greater skill, more determination, better luck, and took advantage of friendly farmers and ranchers.

Many questioned whether the race was worth it. Overall, it fulfilled a major goal of the organizers – a barrage of publicity for the Air Service. The newspapers, both national and local, dramatized the race even before it began, and continued giving it multiple stories each day, including photos and even cartoons. Local leaders, ordinary folks, and neighborhoods across the country joined in the excitement by creating airfields, providing housing and feeding the pilots.

The major criticism of the race focused on the deaths: seven during the actual Race, and nine if you counted the pilots who died while they were flying to the field to enter it. That was a high number of deaths for a peacetime event. The organizers countered by saying deaths were to be expected and experienced pilots knew how to handle "dead stick landings" when the motor failed. Lt.Col. Hartney believed that there was "less danger in aeroplaning than in fast or careless automobiling," and that air crashes were just receiving more press.[5]

The official report of the "First Transcontinental Reliability and Endurance Test," was published by the Air Service in February 1920. Most readers of the report immediately turned to the chapter on accidents and deaths to see how many there had been and the reason for them. It was a shocking revelation: 54 wrecks and crashes, with only 12 of these able to be repaired so that the pilots could continue. The major causes were: motor trouble (29), bad landings (16), unfavorable weather (five), pilots losing their way (two), taking off (one), and burned on the ground (one).

Pilots were blamed for poor landings and becoming lost ("no excuse" said the report's authors).[6] This incredible accusation ignored the fact that pilots had received poor or faulty directions, inadequate maps, and that some landing fields were not long or wide enough and had uneven terrain. Rain and high winds caused problems not only with vision but damage to the propellers. Fog was a persistent problem. The control stop commander at Omaha reported that Captain R.N. Francis in his Martin bomber couldn't find the field because of thick fog, and crashed when he attempted to land. Lt. L.S. Webster wrote that, "on many landing fields the markings were obliterated by rain and not replaced until complaints were made by pilots...I failed to find Herring Field (Des Moines) because of lack of field markings and landed in stubble field rolling through a two-wire fence."[7] Webster also explained that a mechanic had made a serious error by putting too much oil in his plane which caused the motor to stop soon after taking off at Omaha.

He was able to make a safe landing, but it took two hours to drain out "a gallon and a half of surplus oil and clean the spark plugs."[8]

Problems with the construction and maintenance of the planes were legion. Besides frequent propeller damage and the stopping of the engine in flight, "Oil lines, pistons, gas pumps and water connections broke and required repair. Landing gear...needed replacement. Tires blew out....Water pumps froze. Radiators had to be soldered."[9] Yet, instead of pointing to the design of the DH-4 in particular, or egregious maintenance mistakes at control stops, the blame was shifted to the pilots. The authors of the official report claimed that two of the seven deaths, those of Maj. Crissy and Sgt. McClure, were caused by the airmen themselves, Crissy because he was inexperienced in the DH-4, and McClure for putting himself in harm's way to protect the pilot. There are conflicting accounts of Crissy's accident, which killed him and his mechanic, Sgt. Virgil Thomas. It may have been caused inadvertently when Thomas climbed onto the fuselage to help Crissy in the difficult landing, or perhaps because Crissy was unfamiliar with the DH-4. The report failed to recognize these discrepancies. As for Sgt. McClure, the report stated that "If Sgt. McClure had not attempted to climb out of the cockpit no fatality would have occurred."[10] This ludicrous statement ignores the bravery of McClure in his attempt to save the life of the pilot, Maj. Sneed, by trying to climb onto the fuselage of their Le Père aircraft to steady the plane for landing in a muddy field. Furthermore, in a surprising admission of ignorance, the report of the Chief of Engineering claimed that he had never received any information about the DH-4 nosing over in soft ground until he heard of Reynolds' life being saved by his copilot, Lt. Baz Bagby.

There is no doubt that men and women in competitions take risks, and some "blame" could be placed on the foolhardy decisions of men who had little or no experience flying in gale winds, snow and ice. But the participants in the Air Race faced enormous challenges beyond their control. Many of the problems were caused by the inadequacies of the DH-4 and hazardous weather. The planners of the race had given no thought to the potential dangers of snowstorms and ice forming on both the plane and the pilot; under those conditions flights should have been cancelled until the weather improved. The race put the lives of over 100 airmen in jeopardy. Admittedly, the Weather Service had suggested an October 1 start, but more time was needed to prepare the fields for a safe landing. Even postponing the start for a week was not sufficient time to make all the fields safe. The dangerous weather blew in to the East Coast October 9, endangering the aviators leaving from Long Island. The race proved that the Air Service was not ready for such a large-scale effort. The committee had tried to set up safeguards, but more time and training were needed for control stop commanders and field personnel. An evaluation of what equipment and spare parts would be needed at each control stop should have been made. At a minimum, a staple of propellers with protective covers should have been at each airfield.

Otherwise, the authors of the Air Service report gave a fair and detailed account of what had been learned and what needed to be changed. In defense of the race they wrote that the test was "designed not only to show the potentialities but to reveal the problems" of air travel.[11] Lack of parachutes was not mentioned until page 33 of the 35-page report.

The plane with the best reviews was the single cockpit SE-5; the plane with the worst was the DH-4.

A year earlier, in July 1918, an article in *Scientific American* discussed the hazards of flying in fog and above the clouds: "In landing it is impossible for the airman to know whether he is slightly ascending or descending...There are no landmarks in the air." Even the compass had problems. The report acknowledged these difficulties and emphasized that the propeller caused more concern than any other article on the plane, and that "some kind of protection against rain" would have to be solved "before commercial aviation will be a success."[12] Even capping propellers with copper did not help, since the casing flew off. "Rain drops acted as bullets," reported the *Monthly Weather Review* of August 1919. During the race, as a result of heavy rain out of Buffalo, two inches had worn off the tips of the propellers of Capt.

Cement arrows pointing way to air field for U.S. Postal Service. Courtesy of Dppowell.

Donaldson's SE-5 and one inch off the side.[13]

Critics of the Air Race emphasized that it was a "rush up job" scheduled to occur before Congress met, and therefore put airmen unnecessarily in great danger. In a particularly damning summary, one critic claimed that all of what had been learned would have been possible without such a loss of lives and destruction of planes.

In spite of the negative criticism, the Air Service report was beneficial to the fledgling air delivery of mail which had begun in May 1918, before the Air Race occurred and had involved a round-trip flight between New York and Washington D.C., with a stop midway in Philadelphia for refueling and exchange of planes and/or pilots. Congress had appropriated $100,000 for such a route. The pilots were at first from the Air Service, but the U.S. Postal Service soon took over, providing both planes and pilots. After an initial combination of train and air from New York to Cleveland to Chicago in 1919, a transcontinental route was opened a year later from Chicago west to San Francisco. Utilizing the information learned from the Air Race, the field stop at Salduro, Utah, which had given pilots nightmares, was not included. Radio stations at each field were established for weather information, and beacon lights between the fields made night flying a possibility. Ironically, the airplane of choice was the DH-4. Armed with knowledge of its shortfalls, it was modified for safety and remodeled to hold mail. According to postal historian Edward A. Keough, problems with the Liberty engine stopping in flight were resolved with "rigid inspection, servicing and overhaul methods, [and] actual forced landings on account of motor trouble became a rare occurrence."[14]

Had the race convinced members of Congress to support General Mitchell's plan for a separate Air Service? Mitchell testified before the House and Senate, and by all accounts was a dramatic and convincing speaker. But some in Congress, influenced by flashy and fatal barnstorming and Flying Circus events, found it hard to take flying seriously, while the majority reflected the mood of the country and did not want to hear Mitchell's message of the possibility of another war or provide funds. The older generals and the Secretary of War, Newton D. Baker, were not swayed by his arguments for a separate Air Service. General Pershing's comment before the race was telling: "An air force acting independently can of its own account neither win a war at the present time nor, so far as we can tell, at any time in the future."[15] The race itself did little to change this assessment. Lt. Col. John Reynolds and WWI ace Eddie Rickenbacker both testified in December to no avail, and in 1920 Congress cut the budget of the Air Service.

With this devastating blow, Mitchell had a number of options: lay low, bide his time, be social with Washington elites, give parties, be gracious; or begin organizing, and announce to the press another dramatic show focusing on the capability of the Air Service.

Anne Robertson in her high school graduation dress.

10

AFTERMATH

*F*OR TWO MONTHS after Congress's decision not to support the Air Service, Mitchell displayed no outward show of disappointment, resentment or anger. Instead he flew "almost daily, went ice skating, jumped his horses, [and] went trap shooting."[1] He also continued speaking before Congress, and gave the graduation address at West Point to great acclaim. Then, in February 1920 he changed his tactics from warning that the country should prepare for an offensive air war, to one of defending the country in case of an attack. At a congressional hearing, he brought "charts and diagrams to give a vivid picture of an invasion of the United States by hostile fleets."[2] The *New York Times* announced that Mitchell "DECLARES AMERICA HELPLESS IN AIR WAR." He had devised a new plan which would require assistance rather than resistance from the Navy. He needed the Navy's cooperation to provide surplus ships so that he could demonstrate the capability of planes to disable or destroy them from the air. Baz and others from Langley Field were to be part of a dramatic and colorful plan to bomb ships in Chesapeake Bay, and off the Cape near the mouth of the Bay.

Baz's personal life also took a dramatic turn after he returned from the Air Race. He didn't have horses to jump, but he, too, was flying almost daily, trying aerial tricks to impress a young woman, Anne Robertson, who lived and worked in Washington D.C., an hour away by plane from his base at Langley Field, Virginia. Baz's log in November shows a freedom that he didn't dare express in the race, illustrating both his desire for excitement and a lack of fear. "Dropped 2000 feet in 4 turns in tail spin," and "vertical bank at takeoff." His log continued to use a number of French terms that he had picked up while flying in

a French escadrille, such as "did a couple of turns in 'vrille'" (a spinning nose dive), or "tour de piste" (a tour around the field). Some of
these aerial displays occurred in Washington. Anne was not mentioned
in his letters home but there is a revealing hint in his log when he
described doing "spin and low stuff" in the capital "above Lanier
Place"—Anne's address.

When Baz returned from the Air Race he had immediately reported
to the U.S. Air Service Headquarters in Washington where he learned
that his resignation, written before the race, had been accepted. But Lt.
Col. William Sherman successfully talked him into remaining at least
until February, "by which time the separate Air Service bill will be
through Congress." He was promised increased rank and pay and greater
responsibility. He then stayed for five days in Washington, probably to
see Anne.

Baz had first met Anne Robertson in her hometown, Kansas City,
Missouri, before he went to MIT. His William Jewell College football
team played a game there and he stayed with a relative he and Anne
shared through marriage. Anne, still in high school, was five years
younger. He walked her to school in spite of her older sister Mary's
warning to him that Anne was a "flirt." They may have seen each
other again at his brother's home in Washington after WWI, when Baz
was assigned to Langley Field in September 1919, a month before the
Air Race. Anne was now in her early 20s, a sophisticated, outgoing,
and pretty young woman whose job was Assistant Woman's Page Edi-
tor for the *Washington Herald.* As a result of her job she was invited to
many Washington society events, and she described them on the
Women's Page for the *Herald* as well as the *Daily Garment News.* At
one of the dinner dances at the staid Washington Hotel, Anne, who
had a contagious, lively personality, was told by the authorities to stop
"shimmying."

In February 1920, newly promoted Capt. Baz Bagby was sent on a
short assignment to Pensacola, Florida. There he wrote Anne's name
in the sand and then photographed it from the air. It was Valentine's
Day. When he named his DH-4 "Virginia Lee," Anne's pen name at the

Herald, there was little doubt that he was smitten.

That spring one of Anne's columns discussed the proper behavior for unmarried couples in the city park. The headline read: "Lovers, Answer This! Is It Wrong To Kiss In The Park?" The article dis-

TOP: Engagement photos of Anne Robertson and Baz in frame made by Baz. BOTTOM: Steps in park where Baz proposed to Anne Robertson.

cusses the consequences of a Washington Park cop, who, seeing this sort of activity, could charge a couple with "disorderly conduct." Her advice was that kissing should be an intimate and sacred rite, never performed before third parties. Ironically, unlabeled photos in Dad's photo book show steps in a park, no doubt the steps where my dad courted and proposed to her. Did he not kiss her?

Baz's flight log showed that the life of a pilot was one of continual risk. On March 8, 1920, the "motor broke a connecting rod and caught fire...[I] side slipped until the fire was out, landed in an old watermelon patch. Turned over. Broke one strut only!" Eight days later the "linen tore off one end of the propeller and vibrated so that we came down without using the motor." On numerous flights he was doing tailspins, half rolls, and loops (sometimes inadvertently spilling oil on himself) and purposeful stalls. In April, he did some vertical turns to wave at Anne in Washington. When flying in the rain in July, he "landed in a hayfield, knocking down eight fence posts and some barbed wire" but the plane was not damaged.

Anne's boss, worrying about Baz's shenanigans in his plane, told her to "marry that heartsick aviator before he kills himself." Their wedding took place the following September in Kansas City, Missouri. The newlyweds settled in the Officers' Quarters at Langley Field and Baz took Anne on her first plane ride three weeks later. It was a social time at Langley, with dinner parties and dances, and golf planned for the weekends. Anne did not know how to play golf; Baz did not know how to dance. He was relieved that other officers, including Billy Mitchell, jumped at the chance to sign up on Anne's dance card and twirl her around the dance floor under the loving eyes and beaming smile of her proud husband.

Baz participated in several flights for movies, and at Christmas time, 1920, he brought Santa Claus in a plane filled with presents for the children at Langley. When he left with Santa bound for the North Pole the children waved until the plane was out of sight.

The Navy responded to Gen. Mitchell's suggestion of bombing a warship by having their pilots bomb an obsolete ship, the U.S.S. *Indiana* in the Chesapeake Bay on November 1, 1920. This was accomplished with dummy bombs, plus underwater charges. It effectively broke up the ship and there were pictures to prove it, but the Navy brass tried to keep it quiet until the London *Illustrated News* published the photos. It was suspected, but not proven, that Mitchell had given the photos to the English newspaper. With the news out that planes could suc-

Baz in the cockpit of his DH-4 now showing Anne Robertson's pen name "Virginia Lee."

cessfully bomb ships, the Navy, with prodding from Congress and the press, agreed to provide further ships and to bomb in steps: from a submarine, to a destroyer, to a cruiser and then to the largest, a battleship.

Sinking of German battleship *Ostfriesland*. U.S. Air Force.

Mitchell knew that if he were to be successful, he would need well-trained pilots who could bomb accurately so that no Navy or Army brass could question the results. His pilots trained daily. Baz participated in simulated bombing runs first with dummies and then with actual 100-pound bombs from mid-January to early May 1921. His targets were first rowboats in the marshes of Langley Field and progressed to the rusty hulk of the USS *Indiana*, the remains of which were still in Chesapeake Bay. Baz's preferred plane was an SE-5, and often his plane was in the lead. He began hitting the targets in April. His last raid was May 2, 1921, when he made four hits on the target. Baz resigned from the Air Service in May to take a chief engineering job in Iowa.

Mitchell's idea that planes could sink large battleships continued to be resisted by both the Secretary of War and the Secretary of Navy who considered the concept preposterous. Tempers ran high. "That idea is so damned nonsensical and impossible that I'm willing to stand on the bridge of a battleship while that nitwit tries to hit it from the air," declared Newton D. Baker, the U.S. Secretary of War. Secretary of the Navy, Josephus Daniels, had a similar response: "Good God! This man should be writing dime novels."[3] Nevertheless, joint Army-Navy flights continued bombing runs off the Cape, sinking first an ex-

German submarine in June, followed by the USS *Iowa*, then an ex-German destroyer and an ex-German light cruiser. On July 21, it was time for the bombing of the battleship by the U.S. Air Service. It was a well-attended event with 50 reporters, and guests including senators, congressmen, and the Secretaries of War, Navy and Army. On the transport ship the *Henderson*, over 300 people had gathered to watch. Eight battleships held more observers. When the Air Service sunk the German battleship *Ostfriesland* in 22 minutes on July 21, it was to the dismay and disbelief of the Navy brass as well as Gen. Menoher, Mitchell's boss. Reporters observed their "tears and sobs." The press praised Mitchell, and the *New York Times* referred to the event as "an epoch-making performance," while the *New York Tribune* said: "When the subject is calmly considered the Navy will awaken to the truth."[4]

By then, Baz had resigned from the Air Service. He was delighted to read about the successful bombing of the battleship, but even more delighted to have a satisfying job as chief engineer for a manufacturer in Cedar Rapids, Iowa. He easily gave up the glamour and excitement of his forays in an SE-5 for a steady job in middle America. He said that he wanted to live in a world where promotions and assignments were based on one's ability, not on seniority. In Cedar Rapids, Anne learned how to play golf, and together they won a silver vase for first place in a couples' tournament. A few years later he would start his own company, Bagby Engineering Company, in Chicago.

In 1923 John Reynolds was working as Mitchell's second-in-command after a stint in 1922 as commander at Kelly Field, Texas. In August, he and Mitchell flew in formation with 21 planes (Martin bombers and DH-4s) into Bangor, Maine, landing in a hayfield. Mitchell spoke to the Bangor Rotary Club, impressing the mayor and townsfolk with both the necessity and ability of pilots from Langley to defend the East Coast in case of enemy attack. Mitchell took advantage of every opportunity to push his ideas and to garner supporters.

In the meantime, flying became safer for transcontinental pilots after 1924, when the U.S. Postal Service placed beacons along the route and supplemented them with large cement arrows, 50–70 feet long, pointing to major and emergency landing fields.

Despite these improvements, flying continued to be a high-risk profession. Half of the winners of the Air Race died in aerial competitions. In 1922 Belvin Maynard, acting as a minister instead of a pilot, officiated at a marriage ceremony in a six-passenger Fokker at 1500' elevation. The ceremony was broadcast on the radio, and Maynard's questions and the couples' responses could be heard below. At the conclusion of the ceremony, the bride threw her bouquet over the side of the plane. Just a few weeks later Maynard died in a Flying Circus event in Virginia. Alexander Pearson, the round trip winner, also died in a crash while practicing for the 1924 International Air Race. Prior to his fatal accident Pearson had shown his determination and stamina in 1921 by walking across northern Mexico for six days after an emergency landing. He also completed the first aerial survey of wind currents in the Grand Canyon and set the world speed record in 1923. Another Mackay Trophy winner, Capt. John Donaldson, the World War I two-time escapee from a German prison camp, died in a flying stunt in 1930.

Felix Steinle, one of two recipients of the 1919 Mackay Trophy who didn't finish the race in time, was among those Air Race pilots who beat the odds. He retired from the Air Service in 1921. In 1929, he was Operations Manager of a small airline, National Parks Airways, delivering airmail and passengers in Montana, Utah and Idaho. The airline was bought out by Western Airlines in 1937. During all this time Steinle continued to wear the wristwatch that he had received in the New York–Toronto Air race of August 1919. We know that the accident-prone Gish also beat the odds, eventually retiring to Florida.

Encouraged by the support of the news media and believing his arguments were sound, Mitchell wrote a letter to Gen. Menoher explaining what the Army needed to do to be prepared for a future war. His opinions and behavior so irritated his boss that Menoher sent the letter to Secretary of War John W. Weeks. But Weeks supported Mitchell. Menoher was replaced, not by Mitchell, but by another non-flying officer, General Mason M. Patrick, who had been a West Point classmate of Gen. John J. Pershing. Patrick made it very clear that he alone would be issuing orders. Mitchell was purposely sent away on fact-finding tours in Europe and the Far East to keep him out of Washington, yet his often alarming reports of countries increasing their air power for a future war stirred up more controversy. After he completed his five-year assignment as head of operations, he was reassigned to Texas and demoted to Colonel. His ominous predictions of another war continued, including the incredibly prescient warning of a surprise attack by Japanese airmen at Pearl Harbor on a Sunday morning at 7:30 a.m. His ideas, based on his tours of Asia in 1909 and 1924, simply infuriated the old guard, who were already annoyed by his aggressive arguments. Additionally, they were irritated that he didn't dress in regulation clothing but instead wore jackets without the high (and uncomfortable) regulation collar. His clothes, designed and fitted by tailors, were smart and stylish taking advantage of different styles and materials. (At one point, he had also met his staff in his office wearing natty golfing clothes.)

In September 1925, after the loss of three seaplanes between the West Coast and Hawaii and the crash and loss of a Navy dirigible in Ohio, Mitchell lashed out at the "incompetency, criminal negligence, and almost treasonable administration of national defense by the Navy and War departments."[5] That was the last straw for President Calvin Coolidge: Mitchell's court martial was set. The judges would be generals who had never been in an airplane. Mitchell actually looked forward to the trial, believing he would be exonerated. It was a struggle between the old ways, espoused mainly by old men, versus new ideas and younger men. During the seven-week trial, a young officer, Douglas MacArthur, was on the Board. Although it was a secret ballot, someone retrieved the ballot papers and recognized the handwriting of MacArthur, the only one who had voted in support of Mitchell, confirmed years later by MacArthur himself. There was a similarity between the two men: both defied authority when they believed they knew best.

In December 1925, Mitchell was convicted of making "insubordinate" statements and sentenced to five years suspension of rank and reduction in pay and command.[6] He resigned soon after. Officers in the

Air Service who had testified for him: WWI ace Eddie Rickenbacker, Major "Hap" Arnold (future head of U.S. Army Air Corps), Major Carl "Tooey" Spaatz (future head of the U.S. Air Force) and New York Congressman Fiorello LaGuardia (future mayor of New York City) all called for his vindication, but the sentence held.[7]

Earlier that year Major General John Hines, Chief of Staff of the U.S. Army, had appeared before the President's Aircraft Board, and was

Col. Mitchell with wife, Elizabeth, arriving at Emory Hall for court martial, 1925.

Col. Mitchell's court martial. Library of Congress.

asked about the comparative value of reconnaissance by the cavalry and the Air Service. He replied, "In my opinion, the airplane is never going to take the place of the cavalry."[8] Two years later in 1927, Charles Lindbergh, a former barnstormer, became a sensation when he flew across the Atlantic. Yet the negative views of a military air service did not change. In 1934 Secretary of War Baker stated, "The idea that aviation alone can control sea lanes, or defend the coast, or produce decisive results in any other general mission contemplated under our policy are all visionary, as is the idea that a very large and independent air force is necessary to defend our country against air attack."[9] Long-held ideas don't yield easily, and the longer they're held and repeated, the act of giving them up, even if they are ridiculous, can mean a loss of self-dignity. Years later the American psychologist Abraham Maslow (1908–1970) expressed this succinctly: "If the only tool you have is a hammer, it is tempting to treat everything as if it were a nail."

Mitchell was eventually vindicated, but he never knew it. He died in 1935, before his crusade for an independent Air Force was accepted by the military old guard, the Congress and the President. Only in 1938, after the Nazi Anschluss and Hitler's speech at Nürnberg, did President Roosevelt increase production of aircraft in preparation for war. It also helped that "Hap" Arnold, who had been in charge of the Presidio Air Field during the Air Race and was a long-time proponent of a strong air force, was made Chief of the Army Air Corps (the new name for the Army Air Service).

In 1941, when Japan bombed Pearl Harbor, my father was not surprised. He had already expressed his concern about Japan to the *Cedar Rapids Evening Gazette* in a June 4, 1921 article: "Japan, with a well organized air force could bomb our coast cities, destroy our fleet and terrorize the country generally."

Capt. Baz Bagby, age 49, out of the service for 20 years and by now a father of four (ages 10, 11, 15, 18) volunteered for the Army Air Corps in 1942 and was promoted to Major. For many of Dad's decisions including this one, we would hear Mom say with humor: "He's old enough to know better." We went as a family to see him off from Chicago. Another family was also saying goodbye to their father, and they were all crying. My family in contrast was proud and upbeat, and gave Dad a rousing farewell. In truth, none of us realized how hard it was going to be for all of us, particularly my strong, witty and competent mother. During the war, she successfully ran a segment of Dad's business, where she endured demeaning comments about women. Some dinner parties were now couples only, and well-meaning, simpering women would say to me how lonely it must be for her, having her husband overseas and in danger. Irritated at their pitying attitude toward both myself and my mother, I defended her as not being lonely and not missing my father. Fortunately, someone told this to my mother, and Mom understood and forgave an immature child who would rather ruin her mother's reputation than have her be pitied.

Dad left Chicago for Dayton on a commercial plane and then flew in a military plane to Washington. His flying logbook records his first flight with the U.S. Army Air Corps: "April 27, 1942. 2:30. 7000.' Pilot Major Miller. BC-1 from Dayton to Bolling [Washington]. A gas eater. Bumpy over Ohio River."

Lt. Col. Jimmy Doolittle (Baz's friend since WWI) requested that my father accompany him on his secret upcoming raid over Japan (memorialized in the book and film "Thirty Seconds Over Tokyo"), which occurred just four months after the bombing of Pearl Harbor. The planes flown were B-25s, named "Mitchells" after Billy Mitchell. The raid was successful in bombing munitions factories and naval bases in four major towns, but the plans for landing the bombers afterward sadly went awry as planes ran out of gas and many crashed. Baz was flattered to have been considered, but since he knew little about modern planes, it was fortunate that the paperwork did not come through in time for this dangerous assignment. Eventually he was put in charge of the Troop Carrier Command, serving in Africa; and was subsequently involved in the Italian campaigns, providing for rapid troop movement to scenes of conflict and for glider transport to battle areas. Later he was appointed to Eisenhower's staff.

Another Air Race pilot, Colonel Lowell Smith, the first to return to San Francisco in the race, served stateside in WWII as second in command at Davis-Monthan Air Force Base for B17 and B24 crews in Arizona. He had had a distinguished career as the first to refuel in flight in 1923 and the first to make an around-the-world flight in 1924. He held air records for speed, endurance and distance, and received the Mackay Trophy twice. John Bartholf, the pilot who went to the Harvard football game during the race, served in WWII as a Brigadier General stationed at the headquarters of the 3rd and later the 4th Army.

Two other Air Race pilots, Emil Kiel and Carl Spaatz (now spelled with two a's)[10] who had had a testy relationship during the Air Race, saw combat in WWII. Keil was a Brigadier General with the 4th and 8th fighter command. Spaatz's illustrious career included Commander of the 8th Air Force in Europe, Commanding General of the 12th Air Force in Africa, Deputy Commander of the Mediterranean Allied Air Forces, and Commander of all U.S. Strategic Air Forces first in Europe and then in the Pacific. He progressed through Brigadier General to General. None of Spaatz's biographies mentions his participation in the Air Race. My father and Spaatz had had no contact during the Air

Race, but interfaced frequently in North Africa, Sicily, England and France. Baz played poker with Spaatz, and at lease twice Spaatz requested that my father be placed on his staff, but Baz was needed elsewhere. Their personalities were not similar. Baz had the advantage of being able to risk going against the rules because he was not a career officer and he could and did ignore protocol. Spaatz's executive officer was a woman—Baz's much younger sister, Major Sarah Bagby, a WAC. From 1943 to 1946 she handled Spaatz' correspondence and attended and took notes at top-secret meetings. She also acted as his hostess, and played bridge with General Eisenhower. Sarah Bagby's love interest was a lawyer, Major John Dry, whom she had met in 1943 on a ship when both were heading to Europe to their respective assignments. Spaatz gave Sarah away at her wedding in 1946 in St. Louis, Missouri. We were all there, including Dad.

Col. Baz Bagby (left) with staff member in front of his 51st Troop Carrier Command office in North Africa, January, 1943.

As Chief of Staff of the XII troop carrier command, Baz flew in the invasions of Sicily and mainland Italy in 1943, carrying paratroopers or towing gliders. (His interest in the use of airborne troops dated back to 1919 when Brig. Gen. Mitchell first proposed their use.)

He wrote to his son Jamie, my younger brother, about the invasion of Sicily:

Baz's sister, Capt. (later Maj.) Sarah Bagby, is flanked by General Dwight D. Eisenhower and Lt. Gen. Carl Spaatz. Baz is smiling in the background.

We were waiting for a moonlit night and eating lots of carrots so that we could see better...We were over Sicily and the Roman candle guns started up again. This time they were close and I was thinking 'Jamie told me to fight hard' when wham! One of the shells came in through the floor and it meant to go off inside the plane but it didn't go off until it hit the top and there it made a big hole and the wind howled through the hole...Some machine-gun bullets came in through the sides and the floor. They sounded like someone was beating against the side of our plane with a flat board. One bullet went through the side and hit a can of peaches. It didn't go into the can, just dented it, and then fell as if it was all tired out...

The general sent for me to come to headquarters and he said I was a brave aviator and he pinned the ribbon of the Air Medal on my shirt and he sent medals to those who were in the plane with me....

But some of the men in my crew didn't come back and they

haven't come back yet, and they don't know about their Air
Medals.
    Now you know how we fight a war. Kiss Mama and Betty
and Julian for me. Lots of love, From Dad.

Dad's log, July 11, 1943, mentions that "23 of our flight of 144 haven't returned."

Dad was sent to North Carolina in November 1943 for a conference on glider maneuvers. Before leaving, he flew with Generals Spaatz and Patton to observe glider operations in Sicily. He mentioned after WWII how impressed he had been with Patton's intelligence.

Tragically, friendly fire downed several troop carrier aircraft during the Sicilian invasion and exposed an additional danger of leaking gas tanks, which caused unnecessary deaths. Baz hoped to redress the gas tank problem, and he followed the proper channels to do so, but was ignored. To get to the conference in North Carolina Dad travelled to Palermo, Brazil, and Washington D.C. where he was able to speak on his own to Maryland Senator Millard Tydings about the serious design flaw in the gas tanks. Senator Tydings contacted Drew Pearson, a well-known newspaper columnist, who exposed the situation without using Baz's name. When it was finally figured out who had spoken to the Senator without permission, my father was ordered to report to the Inspector General for a reprimand, demotion, or worse. When they met it was established that the Inspector General had been a classmate at MIT. They reminisced about life in Boston, touched glasses, and Baz was told, "Don't do it again." The interview was over.

On D-Day, June 6, 1944, still playing by his own rulebook, my father, age 51, on his own chose to parachute with a Pathfinder group before the land and air invasion. The men were dropped off in German-held territory around midnight in order to set up a radar beacon and holophane lights and create a landing field for the 505th Parachute Group. They were to arrive at 2 a.m., followed by 52 gliders at 4 a.m. The young, well-trained Pathfinder paratroopers, strapped tightly in their parachutes in a cold, dark plane were concerned when they found out Dad's age and that it was his first jump. They began giving him advice: "Don't pay any attention to turning half left when I jumped, the propeller blast would turn me ...keep my arms in, head down, and not to start counting till I had left the plane." Someone found him a wool-en skullcap to wear under his helmet. Just before jumping the officer in charge gave the men a pep talk, including rhetorical question, "Are you mice or men?" One parachuter answered,

Baz returns home briefly during WWII. from left: wife Anne, sons Julian (Jay) and Jamie (Jim), Baz, and daughter Betty. Son John was in the U.S. Army.

"Squeak up, men." Baz landed in a hedge, his fall broken by his parachute snagging a tree. After landing and observing the procedure, my father hitched rides and walked most of the 40 miles to the English Channel, where he boarded a Navy ship captained by an Annapolis classmate of his brother Lew's. Then he had to face the music at Eisenhower's headquarters in England, where he gave his firsthand account of the American successes and shortcomings. He was reprimanded by Maj. Gen. Hoyt Vandenberg for going AWOL and then received a medal.[11] His picture and details of the jump and medal appeared on the front page of the *Chicago Tribune* the morning I graduated from junior high school.

Baz's oldest son, John Bagby.

During the Battle of the Bulge in the Ardennes (Dec. 16, 1944–Jan. 25, 1945), the largest battle ever fought by the U.S. Army, Baz flew from Eisenhower's French headquarters at Versailles to Bayeux near the Front, having heard that his oldest son's infantry unit was in trouble. John Bagby, acting as a medic, was stunned to see his father step out of a command car at the Front. Baz had brought with him one suitcase filled with socks and another full of Cognac, which was passed around to the surprised members of John's unit.

The weather was very cold. Seeing John's thin GI-issued jacket and gloves, Dad took off his flying jacket, leather gloves, and warm flying boots and gave them to his son, along with his .45 pistol. He left, shivering, in his son's clothes. Whenever John was recommended for a decoration he received three-day passes for the rear (away from the Front). During these short periods, he began flying lessons with a pilot on his father's staff and received his pilot's license after the war. Baz's other sons, Jay (Julian) and Jim (Jamie) chose the Air Force. Jay was still training as an aviation cadet when the War ended. Jim started his service during the Korean War. As an Air Force Captain and navigator-bombardier he flew B-29s over the Pacific.

In 1945 Baz was loaned Winston Churchill's personal plane, a C-54, enabling Dad to return in comfort from Great Britain and not be bothered with Customs. The C-54 was loaded with fine French wine, VSOP brandy, and Scotch. Some of his staff came with him. In his logbook, he noted that he "slept in the P.M.'s [Prime Minister's] bed." The plane hopped from Great Britain to the Azores, Montreal, Washington D.C., and finally to Chicago. We all toasted Dad's safe return with the brandy. After one sip, I knew I didn't want to be an adult if I had to drink something so terrible. Baz was discharged in October 1945, and immediately returned to the Bagby Engineering Company, now relocated to Evanston.

Mitchell's dream of an air service as a separate branch of the military was realized in 1947, after the conclusion of WWII, when the Army Air Corps became the U.S. Air Force. Its first Chief of Staff was none other than General Carl A. Spaatz. By then, President Roosevelt had promoted Billy Mitchell posthumously to Major General. Everyone now accepted that Mitchell's predictions of a Japanese attack on Pearl Harbor at 7:30 a.m., of another war, and of the winning of that war thanks to air power, had all come true.

My father died in a car accident in June 1961 at age 68. He was on his way to a reunion of WWI pilots and observers at Wright-Patterson Air Force Base in Dayton. He was buried in a small cemetery on a hill in his hometown of New Haven, Missouri. My brother, Jay, swears that a formation of planes with one plane missing flew overhead, ordered perhaps by General Doolittle. Dad's sister, Lillian, expressed what we all knew: "What was so special about your dad was that he loved life."

The broken propeller from his Air Race DH-4 still resides in the basement of the family home in Evanston, 98 years later.

➤ ◄

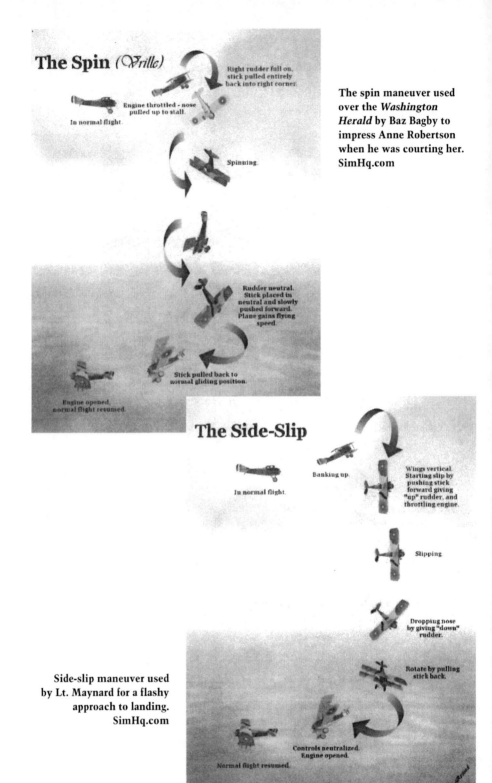

The Spin (*Vrille*)

In normal flight.

Engine throttled - nose pulled up to stall.

Right rudder full on, stick pulled entirely back into right corner.

Spinning.

Rudder neutral. Stick placed in neutral and slowly pushed forward. Plane gains flying speed.

Stick pulled back to normal gliding position.

Engine opened, normal flight resumed.

The spin maneuver used over the *Washington Herald* by Baz Bagby to impress Anne Robertson when he was courting her. SimHq.com

The Side-Slip

In normal flight.

Banking up.

Wings vertical. Starting slip by pushing stick forward giving "up" rudder, and throttling engine.

Slipping.

Dropping nose by giving "down" rudder.

Rotate by pulling stick back.

Controls neutralized. Engine opened.

Normal flight resumed.

Side-slip maneuver used by Lt. Maynard for a flashy approach to landing. SimHq.com

➤ APPENDIX ◄

SYNOPSIS OF SELECT AIRMEN

IN THE TRANSCONTINENTAL

AIR RACE

EASTERN AIRMEN

Bagby, 1st Lt. Ralph (Baz), DH-4
WWI observer with French Escadrille and U.S. Air Service, received DSC. Flew as copilot in race with Lt. Col. John Reynolds, and pilot on the return. Sat on fuselage of plane twice during Air Race to protect pilot. Completed the race.

Donaldson, Capt. J.O., SE-5
During WWI was wounded, POW and escaped, received DSC and DFC. During race flew as low as possible. Major competitor with Maynard. Completed the race.

Hartney, Lt. Col. H.E., Fokker
WWI ace, received DSC. Planned route of race. On return, flew to Long Island "neck and neck" with Baz Bagby. Completed the race.

Gish, 1st Lt. D.B., DH-4
Suffered serious injury in WWI. Checked himself out of hospital so he could race. During race experienced many accidents, never gave up.

Manzelman, 2nd Lt E.H., DH-4
Raced with Pearson and Donaldson. Flew with M.C. Goodnough, his daredevil observer. Completed the race.

Maynard, 1st Lt Belvin, DH-4
Winner of the Toronto–Long Island race in Aug. 1919. Front runner for most of the Transcontinental Air Race. Took shortcuts over mountains and Great Lakes. Dog Trixie flew with him. Mechanical skills of his passenger, Sgt. W.E. Kline, essential. Completed the race.

Pearson, 2nd Lt. Alexander, DH-4
Skillful in icy landings. Used Donaldson's flight pattern as guide. Major competitor of Maynard. Completed the race.

Reynolds, Lt.Col. John, DH-4
WWI commander, received DSC twice. Pilot with Baz Bagby on one way to San Francisco. Returned by train.

Steinle, Capt. Felix, DH-4
Two accidents, needed new plane. Plane burned, mechanic Sgt. H. Myhres pulled him out, broke 3 ribs, continued flying.

WESTERN AIRMEN

Bartholf, Maj. J.C.P., SE-5
Took special care of his plane. When arrived in Long Island asked for permission to go to Harvard football game.

Crissy, Maj. D.H., DH-4
Crashed and died on first day at Buena Vista Field, Sacramento. Field at San Francisco Presidio named after him.

Kiel, 2nd Lt .E.C., DH-4
In competition with Maj. Spatz, arrived before him at Roosevelt Field, Long Island.

Smith, Capt. Lowell, DH-4 Bluebird
First in route east until Cleveland. On return trip plane demolished in fire, took over Spatz's plane. Completed the race.

Spatz (changed spelling to Spaatz) Maj. C., DH-4 Bluebird
WWI DSC. During race competed with 2nd Lt. Kiel. On return trip gave up his plane to Smith.

Worthington, 2nd Lt. R.S., SE-5
One of last to arrive at Roosevelt Field, Long Island. Plane vandalized on return trip to San Francisco. Completed the race.

> END NOTES ◄

CHAPTER TWO

1. Arnold Konheim, "George Washington and Ballooning," *The Digital Encyclopedia of George Washington,* http://www.mountvernon.org/digital-encyclopedia/article/george-washington-and-ballooning/.

2. Herb Friedman and Ada Kera Friedman, "Shot in the Air," *Invention & Technology,* Spring 2006, 26–35. The Friedmans explain how the steam catapult technique is successfully used with planes on aircraft carriers today.

3. John Dos Passos, "The Campers at Kitty Hawk," *Fireside Book of Flying Stories.* Paul Jenson, ed. New York: Simon and Schuster, 1951, 39.

4. www.aerofiles.com/vinfiz.html.

5. *Flying Magazine,* June 1966, 76.

CHAPTER THREE

1. Eileen Lebow, *A Grandstand Seat: The American Balloon Service in World War I.* Westport, CT: Greenwood Publishing Group, 1998, 72–73.

2. Ibid, 22.

3. Ibid, 101.

4. James J. Sloan, *Wings of Honor, American Airmen in World War I: A Compilation of All United States Pilots, Observers, Gunners and Mechanics Who Flew against the Enemy in the War of 1914–1918.* Atglen, PA: Schiffer Military/Aviation History, 1994, 331.

5. Walter J. Boyne, "The St. Mihiel Salient," *Air Force Magazine,* February 2000.

6. Ibid.

7. "1900: The Horse in Transition," International Museum of the Horse, Lexington, KY.

8. Baz's condolence letter appeared in the *Cross & Cockade Journal: The Society of World War I Aero Historians,* Winter 1984, 16.

CHAPTER FOUR

1. Cameron McWhirter, *Red Summer: The Summer of 1919 and the Awakening of Black America*. New York: Henry Holt, 2011, 56.

2. Eric M. Freedman, *Habeas Corpus: Rethinking the Great Writ of Liberty*. New York: NYU Press, 2001, 68.

3. Ron Grossman, *Chicago Tribune* reporter, questioned whether the comment was ever made. August 13, 2013. Jackson himself said it did not occur.

CHAPTER FIVE

1. "Lowell H. Smith." *Nevada Aerospace Hall of Fame*, http://www.nvahof.org/hof/hof-2010/lowell-h-smith.

2. Belvin W. Maynard, "Northeastern North Carolina Stories," northeasternncstories.blogspot.com/2016/03/flying-parson-sampson-county-nc-pilot.html.

3. Herb Friedman suggested that the discarded wires may have been bracing wires such as "Rafwire," an aerodynamically R-shaped bracing wire, used and developed by the English Royal Aircraft Factory, and known to have a performance advantage.

4. "Lieutenant Kiel Gives Observer Thrills in Alighting," *Red Bluff Daily News*, October 8, 1919, 1.

CHAPTER SIX

1. "Patient at War Hospital in Air Derby," *Salt Lake Tribune*, October 14, 1919.

2. "63 Fliers Start 6400-Mile Race," *The New York Times*, October 9, 1919.

3. Belvin W. Maynard, "Northeastern North Carolina Stories," northeasternncstories.blogspot.com/2016/03/flying-parson-sampson-county-nc-pilot.html.

4. Maj. John Bartholf, "From Pacific to Atlantic in an SE 5," *U.S. Air Service*, Vol. 2, November 1919, 14–17.

5. "Pearson Wins Fourth Honors In Air Derby," *New York Tribune*, October 23, 1919, 20.

6. Anthony Paul Martini, "Flying Machines over Zion: Aviation Comes to Utah 1910–1919." *Hill Air Force Base Fact Sheet #10*, 1997.

7. http://pearsoncuratorscorner.blogspot.com/2010_05_01_archive.html.

8. Newspapers reported that Sneed piloted a Le Père; however, in the Official Report of the deaths that occurred in the race, the plane is identified as a DH-4.

CHAPTER SEVEN

1. *Salt Lake Tribune,* October 12, 1919.

2. Belvin W. Maynard, "Northeastern North Carolina Stories," northeasternncstories.blogspot.com/2016/03/flying-parson-sampson-county-nc-pilot.html.

3. "Lt. Maynard Safe at Presidio Field," *New York Times,* October 12, 1919, 3.

4. "Showed Strain of Journey," *The Rome Daily Sentinel,* October 13, 1919.

5. *Salt Lake Telegram,* October 17, 1919.

6. Anthony Paul Martini, "Flying Machines Over Zion: Aviation Comes to Utah 1910–1919," *Hill Air Force Base Fact Sheet #10,* 5.

CHAPTER EIGHT

1. "Two Derby Aviators Killed by Fall," *Salt Lake Tribune,* October 16, 1919, 1.

2. "Obsolete Aircraft," *Chicago Tribune,* October 18, 1919.

3. "Charges Race Casualties to De Haviland Planes," *New York Tribune,* October 18, 1919, 22. Today the DH-4 has a good reputation for longevity.

4. Major John Bartholf, "From Pacific to Atlantic in an SE 5," *U.S. Air Service,* November 1919, 14–17.

5. "Plane Causes Stir Among Uintah [Uinta] Mountain Dwellers," *Salt Lake Tribune,* October 18, 1919; Anthony Paul Martini, "Flying Machines over Zion: Aviation Comes to Utah 1910–1919," *Hill Air Force Base Fact Sheet #10,* 5.

6. Lt. Daniel Gish, "Report to the Office of the Director of Air Service," *U.S. Air Service,* ASNL, November 15, 1919.

CHAPTER NINE

1. "De Haviland Rolls Off Field into Canyon; Rush of Wind Saves Big Plane and Flier," *Salt Lake Tribune,* October 27, 1919, 18.

2. http://pearsoncurators corner. blogspot.com/2010_05_01_archive.html,

3. Major John Bartholf, "From Pacific to Atlantic in an SE 5," *U.S. Air Service*, Vol. 2, November, 1919.

4. Lt. Lewis S. Webster, "Report on New York-San Francisco Reliability Test," Director of Air Service. National Air and Space Museum. Lewis Selwyn Webster Collection (Acct. No. 2010-0041), Box 1, Scrapbook Folder 1 of 4.

5. Maurer, Maurer, "The Flying Game," *Aviation in the U.S. Army 1919–1939*, Washington, D.C.: Office of Air Force History, U.S. Air Force, 1987, 35.

6. "Report on First Transcontinental Reliability and Endurance Test, 1919," *Air Service Information Circular*. Washington, D.C.: Government Printing Office, 1920, Vol. 1, No. 2.

7. Lt. Lewis S. Webster, "Report."

8. Ibid.

9. Maurer, Maurer, "*The Flying Game*," 34.

10. "Report on First Transcontinental Reliability and Endurance Test, 1919." *Air Service Information Circular*. Washington, D.C: Government Printing Office 1920, vol. 1, no. 3, 21.

11. Ibid, 32.

12. Ibid, 29.

13. *Salt Lake Tribune*, Oct. 27, 1919.

14. E.A. Keogh, "A Brief History of the Air Mail Service of the U.S. Post Office Department," http://www.airmailpioneers.org/content/Sagahistory.html.

15. General John J. Pershing quoted in Ron Dick's "*American Eagles: A History of the United States Air Force.*" Charlottesville, VA: Howell Press, 1997, 73.

CHAPTER TEN

1. Burke Davis, *The Billy Mitchell Affair*, New York: Random House, 1967, 66.

2. Ibid.

3. Dave English, "Great Aviation Quotes," http://www.skygod.com/quotes/quotes.html, 17.

4. Burke Davis, *The Billy Mitchell Affair*, 113.

5. Ibid, 218.

6. "Suspension of rank" meant that Mitchell could keep his rank, but lost his privileges associated with the rank and would be unable to advance in rank.

7. Over 75 years later a different interpretation of Mitchell's behavior was described in a 1991 Rutgers PhD dissertation. The author, Michael L. Grummelli, believed that Mitchell's desire to have a court martial was based on his "tremendous arrogance, extreme self-righteousness, gross exaggerations and blatant inaccuracies." Quoted in Philip Meilinger, *Airmen and Air Theory*, 2001.

8. As quoted in Ray L. Bowers, "The Transcontinental Reliability and Endurance Test," *Airpower Historian*, Part 2, April 1961, 100.

9. W.F. Craven and J.L. Cate, editors, "Men and Planes," *The Army Air Forces in World War II*. Vol. 6. Washington, D.C.: Office of Air Force History, 1983.

10. Spaatz changed the spelling of his name from Spatz to Spaatz to satisfy his wife and daughter in hopes that people would be more likely to pronounce it "spots" rather than "spats."

11. The medal was an Oak Leaf Cluster to his Silver Star. Baz's full list of medals and honors includes those from WWI: Distinguished Service Cross, Silver Star with Oak Leaf Cluster, Belgian Order of the Crown, French Croix de Guerre with Palm; and WW II: Air Medal, Bronze Star, French Croix de Guerre with Palm, Silver Star with Oak Leaf Cluster, Commander of the Order of the British Empire, and the French Officer of the Legion of Honor.

➤ ACKNOWLEDGMENTS ◄

*T*HIS TELLING OF the Transcontinental Air Race of 1919 is based on newspaper accounts, U.S. Army documents, my father, Ralph "Baz" Bagby's flying log book of 1918–1945, his letters home to his family from 1917–1920, 1942–1945, and reminiscences of his sons, my brothers, John, Jay (Julian), and Jim (Jamie). Other sources are listed in the references.

I appreciate the help of my brother, Jim Bagby, the historian of the family, who read and discussed many versions of the manuscript with me, located photographs, and corrected errors. Although my brothers and I had different memories of the same event, and different experiences, we all agreed on the courage, strength, compassion, kindness, and sense of humor that we saw in our father.

My heartfelt thanks to editors Carol Tarlow and Abby Wasserman who read various drafts and offered valuable suggestions. Carol was on call for numerous questions and did the final proofing. Abby completed the index. Paul Peterzell and former bush pilot, Charles Vogelheim, instructed me on the craft of flying and terminology. Other readers with a sharp eye included Bill and Linda Kennedy; my cousin, Anne Bagby Pfaff, and her husband, Stuart Pfaff; and Donna Brasset-Shearer.

Nancy Miller, a former student, assisted me in locating some of the newspapers, formated the bibliography and end notes, and proofed an early draft of the book. My husband, Jon, helped with computer problems and photoshopped many of the images, while Fraser Muirhead digitally enhanced key photographs.

The research librarians at the Mill Valley Library provided service with a smile and were always helpful in locating obscure documents. Other librarians at the University of Chicago, San Francisco Library, Marin Civic Center Library, and Monique Campbell of the Niles, Michigan Library, located valuable records. Amanda Williford, curator and archivist at the Presidio Golden Gate, located photographs from Crissy

Field. Molly G. Rawls, Photo Collection Librarian at Forsyth County Library in Winston-Salem, North Carolina, located an important photo of Lt. B. Maynard. Zara Wakeel, a student at Georgetown University, took the photographs of the originals of the race from the collection at the National Archives in Washington D.C.

I am pleased to have had again the skills of designer Beth Hansen-Winter, who was also the designer for my book *Discovering Native People at Point Reyes.*

In addition to my father's letters and log, the most important resources for the Air Race were the newspaper accounts of October 1919. I kept a file of events day by day, compiling articles from many newspapers, which not only provided the story of the race, but also reported other significant happenings of the day. The list of newspapers consulted are included at the back of the bibliography.

Fortunately the first full-length articles I read on the Air Race (by Capt. Ray L. Bowers and Dr. William M. Leary) were excellent and set me on the correct path, as did Burke Davis's fascinating look at Billy Mitchell. Articles featuring Maynard's role in the race by Herb M.F. Friedman and Ada Kera Friedman were also an inspiration, and I was fortunate to be able to talk and correspond with the Friedmans. I also located memoirs of some of the participants of the race which gave a dimension not reported heretofore.

I visited the Mitchell Airport of Milwaukee and viewed their small museum dedicated to General Billy Mitchell. My husband and I also went to the Wright-Patterson Air Force Base (now known as the National Museum of the U.S. Air Force) in Dayton, Ohio, to see the planes flown in the Air Race, as well as in WWI and WWII, including the B25 "Mitchell" flown by Jimmy Doolittle in "Sixty Seconds over Tokyo" in 1942. I found the small Hiller Aviation Museum in San Carlos, California, also valuable. It has replicas of Wright's 1903 plane, the 1911 plane flown by Weldon Cooke, and the "Little Looper" flown by Lincoln Beachey in 1914. The six years spent on research for *A Broken Propeller* were endlessly fascinating.

> BIBLIOGRAPHY ◄

Aerial Age Weekly. May 18, 1922, 210. New York City: Aerial Age Co.

Aircraft: Hearings Before the President's Aircraft Board, vol. 1. U.S. Government Printing Office, 1925.

Almond, Peter. *Aviation: The Early Years.* All photographs from the Hulton Getty Picture Collection Limited. Köln: Könemann Verlagsgesellschaft mbH, 1997.

Bagby, Robert E. *The Bagbys of New Haven, Missouri.* Unpublished, 1971.

Bartholf, John. "From Pacific to Atlantic in an SE 5." *U.S. Air Service,* vol. 2, no. 4, November 1919, 14-17.

Bergquist, David. *Bangor in World War II: From the Homefront to the Embattled Skies.* Charleston, South Carolina: History Press, 2015.

Bowers, Ray L. "The Transcontinental Liability Test." *Airpower Historian,* Part I, January 1961, 45-54, Part II, April 1961, 88-100.

Boyne, Walter J. "The St. Mihiel Salient." *Air Force Magazine,* February 2000.

_____. *de Havilland DH-4: From Flaming Coffin to Living Legend.* Washington, D.C.: Washington Smithsonian Institution Press, 1984.

Brockway, Dr. Robert W. "The Plucky Pioneers of Army Aviation in Hawaii: They earned their flying pay!" http://www.hillmanweb.com/brockway/pioneers.html.

Conover, Harvey. *Diary of a WWI Pilot. Ambulances, Planes, Friends.* Spokane: Conover–Patterson Publishers, 2004.

Craven, W. F. and J. L. Cate, editors. "Men and Planes." *The Army Air Forces in World War II.* vol. 6. Washington, D.C.: Office of Air Force History, 1983.

Davis, Burke. *The Billy Mitchell Affair.* New York: Random House, 1967.

Dick, Ron. *American Eagles: A History of the US Air Force.* Photographs by Dan Patterson. Charlottesville, Virginia: Howell Press, 1997.

Dos Passos, John. "The Campers at Kitty Hawk." *Fireside Book of Flying Stories.* Paul Jenson, ed. New York: Simon and Schuster, 1951.

English, Dave. "Great Aviation Quotes." http://www.skygod.com/quotes/quotes.html.

"Explorers, Daredevils, and Record Setters—An Overview." US Centennial of Flight Commission. http://www.centennialofflight.net/essay_cat/re_category.htm.

Freedman, Eric M. *Habeas Corpus: Rethinking the Great Writ of Liberty.* New York: New York University Press, 2001.

Friedman, Herbert M. and Ada Kera Friedman. "The Great Transcontinental Race." *Aviation History,* November 2010, 50-55.

_____. "The Great DeHaviland Transcontinental Race." Unpublished, 2002.

_____. "Shot Into the Air." *Invention and Technology,* Spring 2006.

Gilbert, Martin. *The First World War.* New York: Henry Holt and Company, 1994.

Gish, D.B. "Report to the Office of the Director of Air Service." *U.S. Air Service, ASNL,* November 15, 1919.

Grider, John McGavock. *War Birds: Diary of an Unknown Aviator.* New York: George H. Doran Co., 1926.

Haller, Stephen A. *The Last Word in Airfields: San Francisco's Crissy Field.* San Francisco: San Francisco Golden Gate National Parks Association, 2001.

Hardie, George Jr. *General William Mitchell, Air Power Pioneer.* Milwaukee: University of Wisconsin, 1970.

Hartney, Harold. *Air Service News Letter.* November 7, 1919.

Herr, Allen. *Wooden Wings Over the Golden Gate: Early Aviation in the San Francisco Bay Area 1910-1939.* Chico, CA: Stansbury Publishing, 2016.

Herris, Jack and Bob Pearson. *Aircraft of World War I 1914-1918.* London: Amber Books, 2010.

Hynes, Samuel. *The Unsubstantial Air: American Flyers in the First World War.* New York: Farrer, Strauss and Giroux, 2014.

Leary, Dr. William M. "Billy Mitchell and the Great Transcontinental Air Race of 1919." *Air University Review,* May–June 1984.

Lebow, Eileen F. *Cal Rodgers and the Vin Fiz: The First Transcontinental Flight.* Washington: Smithsonian Institution Press, 1989.

_____. *A Grandstand Seat: The American Balloon Service in World War I.* Westport, CT: Greenwood Publishing Group, 1998.

Mackworth-Praed, Ben. *Aviation: The Pioneer Years*. Studio Editions, 1989.

Martini, Anthony Paul. "Flying Machines Over Zion: Aviation Comes to Utah 1910- 1919." *Hill Air Force Base Fact Sheet #10*, Chapter 10. 1997.

Maslow, Abraham H. *The Psychology of Science: A Reconnaissance*. New York: Harper & Row, 1966.

Maurer, Maurer. *Aviation in the U.S. Army, 1919-1939*. Washington, D.C.: Office of Air Force History, United States Air Force, 1987.

Maynard, Belvin W. "Flying Parson." *News and Observer* (Raleigh, North Carolina), October 24-31, 1919. (Published by permission of the *Boston Traveller*.) http:northeasternncstories.blogspot.com/2016/03/flying-parson-sampson-county-nc-pilot.html.

McWhirter, Cameron. *Red Summer: The Summer of 1919 and the Awakening of Black America*. New York: Henry Holt, 2011.

Meilinger, Phillip S. *Airmen and Air Theory: A Review of the Sources*. Maxwell Air Force Base, AL: Air University Press, 2001.

Parramore, Dr. Thomas C. "Belvin Maynard: The Greatest Pilot on Earth." www.ncpedia.org/biography/maynard-belvin.

Poe, Edgar Allen. "The Balloon Hoax," *New York Sun*. April 13, 1844. *The Fireside Book of Flying Stories*. Paul Jenson, ed. New York: Simon and Schuster, 1951.

"Report on First Transcontinental Reliability and Endurance Test, 1919." *Air Service Information Circular, vol. 1, No. 2*. Washington, D.C.: Government Printing Office, 1920.

Sloan, James J. *Wings of Honor, American Airmen in World War I: A Compilation of All United States Pilots, Observers, Gunners and Mechanics Who Flew against the Enemy in the War of 1914-1918*. Atglen, PA: Schiffer Military/Aviation History, 1994.

Stoff, Joshua. *The Aerospace Heritage of Long Island (Long Island Studies)*. Interlaken, New York: Heart of the Lakes Publishing, 1989.

"The Tale of the Vin Fiz." www.wright-brothers.org/History_Wing/History_of_the_Airplane/Doers_and_Dreamers/Cal_Rodgers. Dayton.

Trammel, Archie. "The Saga of the Barnstormers." *Flying Magazine*. June, 1966.

United States Air Force Museum. Book of photographs of 140 Airplanes. Air Force Museum Foundation, INC. AMC Branch, Wright Patterson AFB, Dayton.

University of Michigan Center for the History of Medicine. *The American Influenza Epidemic of 1918-1919: A Digital Encyclopedia.* http:// www.influenzaarchive.org/.

Werner, Bret. *Uniforms, Equipment and Weapons of the American Expeditionary Forces in WWI.* Aiglen, Pennsylvania: Schiffer Publishing, Ltd., 2006.

"The Wright Brothers and the Invention of the Aerial Age." *Smithsonian National Air and Space Museum,* acct. no. 2009-0004. https:// airandspace.si.edu/exhibitions/wright-brothers-invention-aerial-age.

NEWSPAPERS AND JOURNALS

Aerial Age Weekly

Army-Navy Journal

Binghamton Press

Brooklyn Daily Eagle

Cheyenne State Leader

Chicago Tribune

Cleveland Plain Dealer

Cornell Daily Sun

Cross and Cockade Journal

Democratic Banner

El Paso Herald

Evening Missourian

Evening Public Ledger, Philadelphia

Great Falls Daily Tribune

Herald Democrat

Huntsville Daily Times

Inter Mountain Globe

Lovell Chronicle

Laramie Republican

Lincoln Evening Journal

Moberly Evening Democrat (Mississippi)

Morning Sun, Binghamton

New Haven Leader

New York Herald

New York Times

New York Tribune

Ogden Standard

Omaha Daily Bee

Philadelphia Public Ledger

Poverty Bay Herald, Australia

Rawlins Republican

Richmond Times Dispatch

Rome Daily Sentinel (New York)

St. Louis Post-Dispatch

Aircraft Journal

Salt Lake Telegram

Salt Lake Tribune

San Francisco Chronicle

Sun, New York

Wyoming State Tribune

Betty Goerke is the author of *Chief Marin: Leader, Rebel, and Legend* and *Discovering Native People at Point Reyes.* She has produced several video-tapes including "Archaeology: Questioning the Past." Betty worked as a field archaeologist in California, Colorado, Kenya, India, and Holland, and taught anthropology and archaeology for over 35 years at College of Marin. She lives with her husband in Mill Valley, California.

CPSIA information can be obtained
at www.ICGtesting.com
Printed in the USA
FSOW01n0921201117
41433FS